HOW TO BE A
HOTTIE

Become Uniquely, Irresistibly You and Attract Men Like Crazy!

HOW TO BE A
HOTTIE

Become Uniquely, Irresistibly You and Attract Men Like Crazy!

Romy Miller

ARTRUM MEDIA

For the Hotties—Past, Present, Future

Paperback ISBN-13: 978-0-9845352-5-5
Paperback ISBN-10: 0-9845352-5-X

Published by Artrum Media.

eBook ISBN–13: 978-0-9845352-6-2
eBook ISBN–10: 0-9845352-6-8

Contents

Why Be a Hottie?

Because hotties get what they want.

In simple terms, that's what being a hottie entails. It's about being the best that you can be. It entails getting what you want, when you want it. It's about being super-confident and allowing all those nagging little voices inside your head to quieten down. You know which ones I'm talking about—the ones that tell you that you're not pretty enough, not cool enough, not skinny enough. The thing about those voices in our heads is that they're nothing more than hindrances to us becoming the hot women we already are.

Being a hottie means being confident and knowing you're worth it. It means knowing that you can do whatever you want to do, when you want to do it. It means knowing you are the best and that the best never takes second best. It means you can get what you want.

Another reason to be a hottie? Because you will be the girl every guy wants to date. You'll be the first girl on their list. And, just so you'll know, you'll be the envy of a lot of other women. That might not be a plus to some, but it comes with the territory.

But isn't that what you want? Don't you want to be that woman that men just go crazy over? Wouldn't it be nice to be able to have your pick of whatever man you desire? Of course, it would. Wouldn't it be nice just to be able to have enough confidence to wear what you want and act as you wish? Yeah, it would!

However, before we go any further, we need to do one thing and that is to define what a hottie is. A hottie is a woman who is cool to hang around with, who loves life and who attracts men like crazy. She is desirable, unique, and independent. She is the woman who can drink beer with the boys and champagne with the girls. She's the woman women want as a best friend and men want as a girlfriend. She is also someone who knows what she wants and isn't afraid to go after it. She is confident, strong and totally open to new experiences. This sort of woman is desirable and *knows* she is desirable. Most importantly, she is confident enough not to hide it.

And that's what this book is about. It's about opening yourself up to new experiences. It's about letting go of an outdated self and stepping into a new one. It's about changing your attitude so you can change your world. And, just so you'll know, it's not exactly about what you wear, but about how you wear it.

The main reason I wrote this book is because I see a lot of women who aren't getting what they want out of life. They settle for second and third best so much it's become their way of life. They get overlooked for promotions and by men who should be happy they'd even give them the time of day. And all this is because of an unnecessary lack of self-esteem. Let me tell you, there is a better way. You don't have to live like this.That where becoming a hottie comes in. It's about having loads of self-esteem and really tapping into your self-confidence. It's about freeing yourself of the things that are holding you back so you can step into a new world. And that world is called being a hottie.

But why would you want to be a hottie? I mean, if men can't see you for the real you and look beyond the obvious, then why bother with any of it? Well, it's not just about how you look. Being a hottie is more of an attitude than a fashion choice. It's not about putting an image out and hoping others will buy into it. It's about actually *being* that image. And all it takes is a little tweaking here and there to get you to that point. If you act like you're beaten down and dejected and have no self-esteem, how is anyone going to see through that?

Also, let's be honest. Every woman wants to be a hottie. Every woman wants to be that woman men really, really like and are drawn to. Every woman wants to be wanted; it's that simple. And so, like I said, becoming a hottie is less of a fashion choice than a state of mind. It's about really freeing yourself of what you've been taught—or taught yourself— and allowing yourself to be open to new things that can enter your life.

Essentially, becoming a hottie is about letting go of the old and letting in the new. It's about being a woman who isn't afraid of having fun while she's searching for her mate. It's about being a woman who doesn't hold back when it comes time to ask—and get—what she wants out of life. It's about being fearless and confident. It's about being sexy and wanted. It's about being a hottie and being a hottie means that you are not afraid to show the world the real and fabulous you.

The true essence of a hottie is about being comfortable with yourself. Once you are comfortable with yourself, you will become—and be—the best version of who you are and just by doing that, you will attract the best men for you out there.

Keep in mind that this book about being a hottie isn't just about dating. Yes, if you follow the advice you will automatically learn to date better, that's a given. However, it's more about becoming the woman that you were meant to be and, once that happens, you will find that you will automatically attract lots of men with little to no effort. Of course, there is some stuff in this book about how to improve upon your existing look, but take all of this in stride because what you are mainly doing is tweaking what you already have, not totally changing it. It's about being who you are but being the best, most self-confident version of yourself.

One last note. While you may not follow all of the advice in this book, just take what you want and use it to your advantage. It's about finding the perfect mix of information that best suits you. Use what you can and disregard the rest, that's my best advice. You, and only you, know what's best for you at any given time. All you need to know that you deserve to be wanted and that you deserve a better life. Yes, you do. Once you feel that, you will start living it.

Ready to get started?

Desirable You

It is one of the best feelings in the world to be desired. (I don't think you will get any arguments from anyone on this.) To be desired and wanted makes you feel valuable. It makes you feel empowered. It can bring a smile to your face and butterflies to your stomach. It can make you blush and make you feel strong. It can make you feel like *somebody*. It can make you feel like you're important. However, before you can really be desired by another, you have to want yourself. I know that sounds slightly odd, but the point is that wanting yourself—i.e. loving yourself—means that you are putting it out there that you are a desirable female who deserves to be attractive to men. In essence, you have to know that you deserve to be desired. Yes, you deserve it. Let me reiterate: Before you can want to be desired, you have to know that you deserve to be desired because if you don't, you'll never feel worthy enough for this to happen.

Let's take a pause and discuss deserving to be desired. More or less, if you don't feel that you deserve to be desired, you won't be. It's that simple. And there are many women who, for whatever reason, think that they don't deserve this. Sure, they read magazines and books that tell them this but it never sinks in. They just never get that before you can feel desired, you have to know in your heart that you deserve it. And you do. Just by the fact that you are a woman, you deserve to be desired and to be treated well. You can't wait for someone to give you permission to do this. You have to give it to yourself. Keep in mind that it's not about what others "allow" you do to. It's about you allowing yourself to deserve it. If you wait around until someone allows you to deserve to be desired, you will be waiting a long time.

I think a lot of women get into funks where they think life has passed them by. I personally know a few. They've given up on it all and continue to hide and seclude and exclude themselves by gaining weight and wearing frumpy clothes. Of course, this guarantees that they will usually find themselves alone on any given Saturday night. How fun is that? (Please note sarcasm.)

In a way, it miffs me that some people just throw their lives away for whatever reason. Sure, life can sometimes suck in a major way, but the point is to get out of the funk and get into the fun. We've all gone through tough times at some point but that shouldn't dictate the rest of our lives. When we let these bad times rule us, we become stuck and getting unstuck can be difficult. But you have to take that first step in order to do so and all that first step entails is you saying that, yes, it would be nice to feel desired. There is so much good stuff to do in life that it just mystifies me that everyone doesn't want to take advantage of it. This may or may not apply to you. If it does, it's time to sit down and get over whatever issue it was that put you in this funk in the first place. If this doesn't apply to you, maybe take a moment and be glad you overcame whatever it was you needed to overcome in order to bring you to where you are.

The biggest hindrance to being a hottie that most women have is that they just stop caring. And when you stop caring, it's hard to get back up on that horse. They just don't think they deserve to be desired. But if you want a better life, if you want to be desired, you have to pull yourself up by your bootstraps, as they say, and go for it. Being a hottie is nothing more than a commitment to go for it. And how do you go for it? You have to take time to really feel what it would be like to be wanted by men. Also, take time to really feel what it would be liked to be wanted by yourself. Yes, by you. If you can just find one thing that you like about yourself, you are on your way because, once you find one thing, other things will pop up and multiply. And when that happens, you rediscover some lost confidence or tap into some new.

I put this chapter in here because I don't think anyone should ever give up on life. I don't care how old you are or what you've done—or not done. You deserve better. Giving up on life and just allowing it to happen around you while you observe quietly is not a prescription for happiness. It should be everyone's goal to be happy. But why? Why be happy? What does that have to do with being a hottie? Everything! Without feeling and experiencing happiness, what's the point? Happiness is a gift that's been given to us so we will continue on with the species. So, if all of us are going around in a funk, feeling like loathsome creatures, our species would probably cease to exist. And we'd all be miserable in the meanwhile. Why would anyone in their right mind want to do that?

Happiness is a very important part of feeling desired. If you can do this, the rest will follow. Confidence will be easier to obtain and people will pick up on your happiness and automatically want to be around you more. Attracting men will be easier, too, mainly because most men want to be around a happy woman. Why? Because they're fun! And everyone loves to be around a fun person. So, allow happiness to be your goal and once you feel happy, you will begin to feel desired because you will start becoming more desired due to your innate happiness.

So, feeling desired is the goal. Once you feel desired, you will *be* desired. But you might have to take that first step on your own. This book will concentrate on getting you to that first step and beyond. And once you're there, you are going to love it. Who wouldn't? Feeling wanted is the best feeling there is. Besides feeling loved, that is. But, maybe, it's one in the same.

And don't run away from it either. I've known women who, after being whistled at on the street, want to run and hide. "Oh, he can't be whistling at me!" Well, maybe he was and he was because you are attractive and desirable. These women think they couldn't possibly be desired because they don't think they deserve it. Learn to accept that men want women and that you are a woman. Learn to embrace your femininity. Learn to love yourself for who you are. And then learn to love others who think you're hot stuff. Because you will be. You deserve it.

Uniquely You

In order to become the best version of yourself or rather the hottie you truly are, you have to become *uniquely you*. But that begs a big question, just what exactly does this mean?

You have to realize that it is not imperative that you change yourself in order to be a hottie. Being a hottie means being yourself. The best version of yourself you can be. So, if you have freckles or muscular legs or whatever, accept that this is part of you. Yes, you need to accept it, love it and revel in it. Whatever it is that makes you uniquely you should be used to your advantage. If your hair tends to be on the curly side, show those curls, and keep in mind many, many women would love to have your hair. Same thing if you have straight hair—embrace it for all its beauty. Becoming uniquely you doesn't mean you have to do a lot of work. It just means you embrace what you already have and build on it, too. By building on what you have, all you do is take your existing natural characteristics—some might call them quirks—and milk them for all their worth. Maybe you're really smart. So, work that. Wear those cool but funky glasses and look like a sexy librarian. Maybe you're really artistic, so work that to your advantage by wearing those cool, bohemian-type clothes. Maybe you're a gymnast, so show off your muscular legs.

The point is to take what you have and work it. But the even bigger point is to take what you have and love it. Use it to your advantage to become uniquely you. Instead of trying to work around something, you work *with* it. And that's how you become uniquely you and that's what will make men flock to you. No one likes a phony, so if you are genuinely you, you will automatically attract men who will want you for you and not some image you've presented to the world in hopes of being accepted more. If you can accomplish this, not only will you attract more men, but you will attract men who will be better for you because you are putting out an honest image of yourself. And this, in turn, will attract more honest men—better men instead of just superficial douchebags.

So, instead of "fixing" what you've got, work with it and use it to your advantage. That's the quickest, sure-fire way to not only attract more men but to be more accepting of yourself. And through self-acceptance comes much self-esteem and a woman with a lot of self-esteem is a woman many men would like to know better.

One last reason to become uniquely you. There are many men who are turned on by what you may perceive as flaws. Say you have lots of freckles on your chest. There are men who really dig this. This goes for all things we, as women, might think of as flaws. Whatever it is, I can guarantee you that there is a man who is turned on by it. Seriously. This is why you must revel in your "flaws" and begin to see them as something that is advantageous. That they are assets rather than liabilities. They are what make you unique and it is much better to be unique than to be just like everybody else.

Perpetual Pollyanna?

One thing that sets confident and desirable people apart is the fact that they can override negativity with positivity. They don't let the negative Nancy's rain on their parade and they don't let anyone cover their silver lining with unnecessary clouds. And while that is a very flowery way to put it, it's true. In essence, they're positive people.

When I wrote one of my other books, *How to Be Wanted*, I wanted to really showcase how your attitude can make or break you. If you're feeling positive, you're more in tune with the world and, if you're feeling negative, you're more out of step. Hotties have fabulous lives because they have positive attitudes and they know that using the Law of Attraction can be very beneficial.

Now, while this book isn't about the Law of Attraction, I do want to emphasize that what you give is what you get. If all you ever give is negativity, then that's probably what you're going to get back. However, if you can turn it around, you can start to see more positive things open up simply by adjusting your attitude. And, you should know, hotties always have good attitudes. If they get down in the dumps, they keep on plugging until they've risen above whatever bad situation that befell them. It's important to just understand that like attracts like. And if you have a positive attitude you will, in turn, attract men with positive attitudes. Being positive can and will bring good results. It can also turn your life around.

I know it's sometimes hard to put a smile on your face like a perpetual Pollyanna, but sometimes that's just what we have to do in order to move forward. While it is important to sort out any negative feelings, it's more important not to get bogged down by them. I know when life throws us curveballs, it's hard not to wallow in the misery. This is normal. But when you keep wallowing and never rise above, then it becomes a problem.

In the end, it's just sometimes best to shut out negativity and reach for positivity. If negativity has become a bad habit for you, take a moment to assess what got you off track and once you figure it out, get back on the right path. Find a way to your bliss. It's waiting for you and once you find it, embrace the hottie you are.

Newsflash: You're Already a Hottie!

Who? You? Yes, you. You are already a hottie. I don't care if you're sitting on the couch in your floppy pajamas watching a rerun of your favorite sitcom or if you're standing in line to pay your water bill. You are a hottie. I don't care if you haven't had a date in God knows how long or even had a guy on the street give you a second look. I don't care what state of disarray your life may or may not be in right now, you are a hottie.

Say it to yourself: "I am a hottie!"

That's the first step you have to take in order to become a hottie. Yes, of course, you may feel a little odd saying that to yourself, but if you can't even say it to yourself, how are you going to project it onto the world? Telling yourself that you are a hottie is of upmost importance. It has to be done. So, say it and be happy you can.

While I want this book to be fun and informative, I do want to get a lot of this nonsense out of the way first. This nonsense that I am referring to is some women's refusal to see themselves as attractive, capable human beings. You know who I'm talking about. Some women, no matter how beautiful they are, will never see their beauty. And we all have beauty, too. Regardless of whether we may or may not have supermodel good looks or ever see our faces on the cover of a magazine, we are beautiful. *Yes, we are.*

So, why can't we tell ourselves this? Why can't we allow ourselves to be the hotties that we are?

The real reason we have trouble telling ourselves how great we are is because there is this societal dictate that forces us to always be humble and never act as though we're better than we are. In fact, we are taught to sometimes act as if we are below everyone else to keep us "humble" and from getting the "big head." This is good on the surface but many times it has a tendency to get misinterpreted. This is when we stop being true to ourselves. As a result of this, many of us go too far in our quest to not offend others and as a result look down on ourselves and never give ourselves the credit we deserve. What happens then is that we level ourselves. Yes, we may be really pretty and smart, but we can't tell anyone that, can we? We might appear to be conceited and then what will others think?

And, hence, the problem.

We become too concerned about what others think. We are afraid of being judged and then we stop being the fabulous people we really are. I mean, what will everyone think if I think highly of myself? Why, they'd think I was just some conceited bitch. They might even call me names! To my face! It's best to hide that part of myself just to make sure no one comes after me. Do you get the picture? These are the thoughts that run through our heads and cause us to act lesser than we really are.

Well, guess what? If someone decides to "come after" you, they'll do it regardless of what you tell yourself. You can't hide who you are. And you shouldn't! Just because you tell yourself how wonderful you are doesn't make you a conceited bitch. You have to remember that you are a wonderful person and if you hide it, no one besides yourself will ever know. You don't have to lord your hotness over everyone, but you don't have to deny it either. Just be yourself and don't try to hide just how great you are.

This is precisely the problem with being a hottie. We think that other people won't like the fact that we're not staying down and pretending that we're less than we are. Other people might not approve. Well, if you want to be a hottie, you have to get over this because this is nothing more than low self-esteem at work. Sure, there are people who will want to talk about how conceited you are and that's because they'll be jealous of you. That's usually the reason anyone talks badly about anyone else—they're jealous. And so what if they are? Who cares?

If you want to truly blossom into the hottie you already are, then you have to get over this notion that you can please others by putting yourself down. You can't. In fact, I'd say you can rarely please anyone other than yourself on a daily basis. Besides, who are these people who want you to look down on yourself? Who cares about them? More importantly, why do you want to please people who are only happy as long as you act less than you are? Why are you trying to please people who would attack you for showing the world just how great you are? These are not people who have your best interests at heart, so why should you try to please them?

In the end, you're already a hottie. However, allowing the world to know about it is entirely up to you. If you want to fully come into your hotness, then you have to, as they say, damn the torpedoes. And then you have to pick yourself up, look in the mirror and say, "Damn, I'm hot! I'm a hottie! And I don't care who knows it!"

If you can do that, you will be well on your way to claiming your place as a hottie. And what else could be better than that?

Empower Yourself to Be a Hottie

Empowerment is the name of the game. So, empower yourself right here, right now, this minute. Empower yourself to be a hottie. Channel your inner hottie and bring her forth. As I said in the last chapter, you're already a hottie, even if you don't think so. *Yes, you are.* You just have allow yourself to become one.

Without some form of empowerment, we, as humans, would hardly be where we are today. We certainly wouldn't have cell phones and internet access, that's for sure. Empowerment means that you are giving yourself the freedom and power to do as you choose. You're allowing yourself to go for what you want out of life. It also means to give someone a greater sense of confidence or self-esteem. Again, why not start with yourself? *Empower* is such a great word and I really want you to get the gist of it.

So, why not begin right now empowering yourself to be a hottie? What do you have to lose? Of course, I don't mean to go buy a slutty dress and some cheap high heels and hit the dance floor. That's not what this is about. What this is about is being able to gain enough confidence in yourself to overcome your hesitancy to show the world just how great you are. Confidence is the main priority. If, however, you are reluctant to take your place in life, then you will not have the confidence to show the world that you are a smart, sexy and empowered woman.

And that is the real reason most women don't—or won't—ever consider themselves hotties. They don't have enough confidence to do so. There's this hesitancy, this inability to commit to it. And this is at heart of the matter. For some reason, we might see it as taking a risk and some of us don't like taking risks. However, in order to gain anything, some risk is involved. And what, really, do you think you risk if you become a bona fide hottie? Your self-esteem wouldn't be at risk. In fact, you'd gain more of it. Oh, I get it. You think you might end up looking like a fool.

But, really, what are the chances of that?

If you know how to act and how to apply yourself in social situations, what are you afraid of? It's just taking that chance, isn't it? Opening yourself up to it, right? Well, there you go. The only thing I can tell you here is that nothing ventured, nothing gained. It's your choice and you call it. But you have to realize that you have to make an effort.

So, empower yourself to be a hottie. Empower yourself to *be* yourself. No one else will do this for you; you have to do it for yourself. Stop hesitating and take that first step into being the most desirable, uniquely you that you can be. Getting over any hesitancy about being a hottie is probably the first—and biggest—obstacle most women face. Why is there this hesitancy? Why do so many women keep themselves down and turn into frumps? I think it's mainly due to perceived expectations. What I mean by this is that some women perceive that others—friends, family, et al—want them to stay in the frump mode and because of their over-eagerness to please they do so. And once this happens, it's hard for them to ever think of themselves as anything else other than a frump. It's hard for them to even begin to fathom themselves as being a desirable woman. It's just not in their realm of consciousness.

How to overcome such an obstacle? Just start telling yourself that you are a hottie and you deserve to be desired. And, yes, it's that simple. It's also the first step in overcoming hesitancy. Because, once you hesitate, all sorts of doubts can creep in to thwart any success you might have. And that's not being a hottie. That's allowing the opinions of others to keep you down. And that's just not cool.

So, hold your head up high, hottie, and allow yourself to become the most empowered, successful, sexy version of yourself that you can be. It's in there. You just have to bring it out. And the first step to bringing it out is accepting yourself and accepting the fact that you have allowed others to form your opinion of yourself. Get over that and you will be well on your way.

Do I Deserve to Be A Hottie?

Before you go any further, ask yourself this question: Do I deserve to be a hottie? I'll answer it for you: Yes, you deserve it. Why wouldn't you?

While I briefly touched on this earlier, I wanted to really reiterate my point so it gets across. You really have to give yourself over to being a hottie. It's a step that can be very difficult for some women because they simply don't think it's within their ability to do it. In fact, they don't think they deserve it. They think that it's something that's beyond them. They think that it's something that only other women deserve. But the thing they need to ask themselves is just exactly how did these other women become hotties? It's because they never doubted whether or not they were hotties in the first place. They simply were. They knew it from the beginning. This is what you have to do—know that you deserve to be a hottie and know that you already are one.

There are many women in this world who, for some reason, are really down on themselves. This self-defeating attitude may come from imperfect childhoods—and I can assure you, many of us have had those—or just a deep-seated insecurity or maybe a combination of both. This is a false perception that needs to be overcome and it needs to be overcome because it will get you nowhere.

But how do you get there? How do you get from A) Not so much a hottie; to B) Hottie Forever? It's easy. You allow yourself to be a hottie.

That might sound simple and a little trite, but it's the truth. By actually acknowledging the fact that you deserve to feel good about yourself, that you deserve to be desired by men and that you deserve to be a desirable person, you can overcome whatever it is that is holding your back. It's that easy. The fact that it is so easy is the reason why it's so hard for so many women to grasp. You are your only obstacle. Use the assets you already have and get to it.

If you're having a problem committing to the process, you need to first figure out why you think you don't deserve it. Most likely, it is simply a lack of self-confidence. Did someone, sometime say some mean things to you that made you feel bad about yourself? Did someone, somewhere in your life make you think that you were worthless or not good enough? Well, that's happened to most people. It's part of life. But you can't let anyone stop you from being the person you were meant to be. You need to ask yourself if you're living the life that you want or are you living the life that others have dictated for you to live. This is why you have to decide for yourself what you want your life to be. You have to realize that you deserve to be what you want.

One thing that might be holding you back is the very fact that you don't want to draw attention to yourself. This comes from being overly self-conscious and is related to self-esteem, or lack thereof. Many women are like this. They feel if they draw attention to themselves then that attention will be bad and will make them feel very uncomfortable. It's about being *too* self-aware. When you become too self-aware, you begin to censor yourself in lots of ways that are just self defeating. When you do this, you are not properly valuing yourself or your place in the world. This is so wrong on so many levels, but mostly wrong because you're basically lying to yourself. Of course you have value! Of course you're wanted! But in order for you to feel it, you must first believe it's true. That's the trick, so don't trick yourself into believing you are any less than you really are.

Ask yourself: Why not me? Why don't I deserve to be a person who is desired? I'd be willing to bet you can't come up with a single good reason why not. And if you do come up with several? Just examine them. I'd be willing to bet they are all rooted in low self-esteem or other people's opinions of you. Low self-esteem can and should be overcome. Other people's negative opinions of you shouldn't dictate anything in your life and are more of an indicator of who *they* really are rather than who *you* really are. And we will discuss how later in the book.

So, yeah, you do deserve to be a hottie.

Other People's Opinions

Keep in mind that, if you're not careful, other people's low expectations of you will dictate the life you live. And what do I mean by this? Let's say you grew up going to a school where all the teachers were always on you about how dumb you were, or, rather, how dumb they perceived you to be. (This is an extreme example, but stay with me.) And, even though your test scores proved otherwise, you believed them. You believed that you were, well, a dummy. So, all through school, even into college, you studied hard and made good grades even though you always felt you were on the brink of failure. But you passed with flying colors time and time again, proving these people wrong. But not once did you ever stop and ask yourself, "Why do I think I'm so dumb? I get good grades, I have a good, well-paying job and I take care of myself. Why do I think I'm an incompetent idiot?" Of course, the answer would be, "Because I was told I was dumb and my low self-esteem would not allow me to believe otherwise."

It's that easy. If you're constantly told that you are dumb, you will always think you're dumb! No matter how well you do on tests or how well you do in life, simply because these people told you that you were dumb and, because you were so young and didn't know any better, you bought into it. If you think you're dumb, you won't try for promotions or better jobs or living abroad or doing anything too overly ambitions. You will stay in your place with your dunce hat placed firmly on your head like the village idiot these people lead you to believe that you are. When, in fact, you are a smart, very capable human being.

This same concept applies to everything you your life. If you are told you are short, unattractive, afraid or whatever, you will probably begin to believe it regardless of whether it's true or not. It's like a virus. Once you start to feel these things, you will most likely become these things. This is why it is so important to be true to yourself and to know and believe what you truly are—a valuable human being.

This goes the same for being a hottie. If others put you down and told you that you're not attractive enough for this or that, it was just their way of keeping you in your place. And they're lying! Learn to recognize the lies in your life and don't give these people the satisfaction of keeping you down.

You don't have to be rich to be a hottie. You don't have to have supermodel good looks, either. You just have to be you and tweak yourself a little here and there in order for it to happen. It's about using what you have already got to your full advantage. It might not come overnight, but it will come. Once you start applying yourself, and because you're just using what you already have and merely being a more confident version of yourself, you will soon realize it will become second-nature. You will wonder why you didn't try it sooner because the life of a hottie is one to be relished. And isn't that what you deserve? A really good, fun and happy life? That's what hotties live. So, why not you?

Indulge in the Lazy

Before we continue, I wanted to touch on a subject that really needs to be mentioned and it needs to be mentioned because it's something we could all use. And what is it? It's a little something called *downtime*.

Most of us are busy all day long. (I can attest to this.) And yet, we never stop to catch our breaths or smell the roses. We get up, we get dressed, we go to work, we come home, we clean the living room and on and on it goes. Never once do we stop and say to ourselves: Damn! I need a freakin' break!

And we do. All women need to take time for themselves. Women who are comfortable with themselves know this. They will blow off things for a massage or manicure. And why shouldn't they? It's ideal to pamper yourself ever so often just so you'll know you're working for something. So, occasionally, I say, indulge in the lazy.

Of course, I don't mean to blow off your responsibilities like work or family or whatever. But things that you can put off or delay? Why not? Why not put them off and have a lazy day every once in a while? Every once in a while, indulge the lazy side of you. (Believe me, once you get married and have kids, this won't be happening too much.) Take the morning or afternoon off to read a sexy novel or go strolling in the park. On Sunday morning, wait to get up and just lie in bed, enjoying the feeling of your sheets and nice duvet. Or get up and go lie on the couch and flip on the TV. Cover yourself up with a throw and relax before you have to get going. Remember how you'd watch cartoons every Saturday morning when you were a kid? Do that again but with things you enjoy in your life now. Take time to watch or do something you like. Regardless, just take time to relax and do nothing. This will reset your brain and rejuvenate your body. This will give you better perspective, as well, and enable you to really go for the gusto when you most need to.

What I really want to emphasize here is that some people get so rooted in their routines that they lose perspective of their lives. They don't see what is really going on in their lives because they are too busy trying to keep up. Time can go by fast and if you're too stuck in a routine, the years can literally disappear. Taking time off will give you that perspective. It will also help you to stay on track with what's important.

The point is that busy, busy, busy means stress and stress means wearing yourself down. It's imperative to take time to indulge the lazy. When you do this, you are rejuvenating yourself. And when you do this, you will truly be able to gain perspective and make the changes you need to become the best *you* that you can be.

Naturally Beautiful

Being naturally beautiful entails just that—looking natural.

The point of being a hottie isn't to have lots of plastic surgery. (Again, we will discuss this later.) But it is to be to be naturally beautiful. This means wearing makeup that doesn't look like you trowled it on. If you look in the mirror and see anything that resembles Bette Davis in *Whatever Happened to Baby Jane*, then you might have a problem. Obviously, this is a joke, but the point is that when it comes to makeup, less is more. Also, when it comes to your overall look, less is more, too.

Let's get to it.

Of course, it's great to get all glammed up when you hit the clubs. However, in your everyday, life, wearing makeup that looks natural is the best route to take. I can't tell you how many men I've heard say that they love a woman who doesn't wear loads of makeup. This is your cue. When a man says he likes something, listen to it. Especially when it comes to makeup. So, if you wish to attract men like crazy, go more natural and use just enough makeup to enhance your natural features. That is what you are after. Just keep in mind that makeup should always be used to enhance, not disguise and you'll be okay.

When it comes to your hair, again it is best to go with your natural color. I know many women who love the blonde from the bottle. But the problem is that many women cannot pull this off. If your skin tone is not exactly right, it can make you look sallow, or older or somewhat unhealthy. Any good stylist can give you tips on this and can also give you advice on highlights and other options as well.

The main thing to look at with hair is that it should look natural and not overdone. Also, men love long hair on a woman. Of course, this doesn't mean growing it to your ankles, but just long enough so they can run their fingers through it. If you have really short hair and love the look, it might be a good idea to girly it up some by wearing headbands or putting in cute barrettes or whatever. The important thing is that whatever accessory you do use, it should go with your look.

One last note on hair. It's a good idea to use as few styling products as possible. Make it as luxurious as you can by paying attention to your hair care and never over-processing. If you hair is currently fried, just see a stylist who can give you tips on how to get it back into shape.

It's also a good idea to look more natural when it comes to your eyebrows as well. Over-plucking is never a good idea and if this is something that you have to contend with, there are now products on the market that can help you grow your natural eyebrows back. Just see a professional and study the risks before you dive in. Natural looking eyebrows will make you look younger and we can all remember how the world went crazy over Brooke Shields's eyebrows when she first hit the scene. So, my best advice is to tweeze a few strays here or there but always leave it to a professional for any waxing. And when you do see a professional, tell them you want to look as natural as possible.

Let's move onto your nails. Again, without beating a dead horse, natural looking nails are great, though sometimes glam polish can look cool, too. It's your call but just keep them a length that doesn't resemble anything related to claws. It's also a good idea, if you're not using polish, to keep them buffed and leave the press-on nails at home. Also, if you do paint your nails, be sure to mind the chips. The ragged, chipped look is never attractive, so just polish over until you can get the opportunity to redo them.

As far as toenails are concerned, most women look great with a cherry red polish on them or, if you prefer, just buffed and trimmed will look great, too.

Lastly, in order to be naturally beautiful, you might consider your scent. Overdoing on perfume, while not a deal breaker, can be a turnoff to a guy. It also interferes with your natural scent, which is what he will be subconsciously attracted to. Sounds gross, but there is a lot to be said for pheromones. Of course, this doesn't mean to opt out on deodorant, but just don't apply so much that all you smell like is clean cotton or jasmine or whatever scent you're currently using. Also, keep in mind, that it might cause some guys to have an allergic reaction.

The most important thing to understand is that men will love you for you not for your make-up or perfume or whatever. That is why it's imperative to always be as naturally beautiful as possible. I think many women hide behind heavy make-up but it's not really necessary. If you have to wean yourself off of it, then start the process. The point is to have enough confidence that you don't try to hide behind a veil of make-up. And once you can do that, you will have the fellas eating their hearts out. Literally.

The gist is that you should be confident being yourself and should never rely on anything to disguise or hide who you are. Makeup, hair color and nail polish are simply meant to enhance and decorate, not to change what you look like entirely. Looking naturally beautiful means using products that make your natural beauty the focus and never disguise it.

Keeping it simple and displaying your natural beauty will not only attract more men, but might just save you time but also bundles of cash. And with that, you can buy more shoes. Not a bad tradeoff, is it?

Accentuate the Positive

I want to take a moment emphasize the main point in becoming a hottie. Basically, you enhance the greatness you already have—*you* don't change. That's why I wrote the chapter on being naturally beautiful. It is imperative to always have the confidence to be yourself. It's necessary to accept what you've got and learn to enhance it rather than totally change yourself.

In essence, you accentuate the positive. And when you can do that, you are going to be way ahead of the game. And you will feel so much better about yourself and that's because you will know that you are genuinely a person who is worthy of being desired.

Being a desirable person is about quality, not quantity. Many women attract guys like crazy, but keeping them is the problem. When you are genuine and you're not so concerned about catching every guy's eye that you run across, you will invariably attract more. And this is because you are authentic. Being authentic means men will automatically be more attracted to you. Essentially, once you stop trying so hard, you will be much more appealing. And, because you are being you, you will begin to attract the right kind of man. When you develop this confidence in yourself, you'll be able to discern what men are worth your time and which ones you need to let pass on by. This is because you know you are a person of quality and quality always recognizes quality, especially when it comes to members of the opposite sex.

Accentuating the positive is about emphasizing your positive features and the best positive features you have is your true self. If you want to be a hottie, it's really not that hard. Like I said, all you have to do is start accentuating the positive be proud of yourself and act like you belong wherever you are. If you want to attract men like crazy, find that lost confidence and tap into it. Let the world know who you are and that you are a desirable, confident woman. Once you do that, you will have to beat them off of you. Which, may or may not, be a bad thing, depending on your attitude.

Stand Tall—Literally

Being a hottie is really about how you carry yourself. Posture is incredibly important if you want to project the correct image of yourself. If you hunker down like you're afraid a bomb is going to hit at any moment, a man will look right past you. They will be drawn to the woman who is walking boldly instead. This is because he knows this woman has the confidence to talk to him if he approaches her. Bad posture can make you look less like a hottie and more like someone who's been beaten down by the world. It spells insecurity and insecurity is never attractive.

If this applies to you, how do you compensate for it? It's so easy, you might not believe me. You simply stand up taller. Yes, that's right. You start practicing good posture. Keep in mind that when people see you, they are looking at your body language, as well. Therefore, if you carry yourself as if you're downtrodden, you will be seen that way. Bad posture will give a bad impression. I say literally stand up for yourself. Throw those shoulders back and hold your head up high. It's an easy fix and if you can start doing this, start expecting some notice. The great thing about this is that the more you do it, the easier it will be. It's simply a matter of forming a good habit.

Bad posture simply means lack of self-esteem. Having good posture tells the world you are not only accentuating the positive, but you are a force to be reckoned with. The good news is that it's not that hard to overcome any issues you have with appearing confident, but you have to be willing to try and get over your hang-ups and become more self-aware. This is when you can start projecting to the world the real you, the desirable you. Many people do things they're not even aware of but then, when it comes to light, they finally understand why they haven't been getting what they want out of life. It's a beautiful thing when that happens. If you can just become aware of the image you are projecting, you can adjust it so that you can let the real you shine through. And that's what the world—and men—want from you. They want the real you, the genuine you, not the you who might be possibly hiding who she really is. This is when you're no longer altering who you are just to fit in. Being yourself is the best thing you can be because once you accept yourself enough to show the world who you really are, you might just find that the world accepts you more.

It's Not What You Wear—It's How You Wear It

This is just a quick note. When it comes to buying clothes, it's not what you wear but how you wear it. You know the old saying, "She could wear a paper sack and still look good?" This is what I am talking about.

Of course, this goes without saying, but I am not telling anyone to wear a paper sack unless they really want to, of course. Kidding aside, you have to find that fine line between you wearing the clothes and letting the clothes wear you. If you can do this, you will look great one-hundred percent of the time.

Some women exude so much confidence it doesn't matter what they wear, hence the paper sack analogy. So, having said that, let me say this. When it comes to clothing, the fit is everything. Your clothing shouldn't be too tight or too loose. It is meant to accentuate your body and make you look good. But looking good shouldn't mean being physically uncomfortable. You do not want your clothes to feel like a second skin. It's like this. If you can't be comfortable in your clothes, then why bother wearing them? It's key to find comfort and style and with the fashions today, this shouldn't be too hard to achieve.

So, whenever you go clothes shopping—or go to your own closet to find something to wear—follow this guideline.

- It's not what you wear; it's how you wear it.
- Your clothes should fit well. They should not be so tight that you look like you've been stuffed in them or so loose that you lose your shape.

- Clothing should feel comfortable. This doesn't mean sweatpants and t-shirts. This means clothes that are stylish that you can move in and won't feel banded in when you sit down or stand up or whatever.
- A little stretch in the fabric makes comfortable clothes but lends itself to the form of a person, as well. It's a win-win for everyone.

Following these short guidelines should help you not only shop better but look more stylish, too. And in the end, you will always feel comfortable in what you're wearing.

One more thing. If you are unsure of what you'd like your style to be about, scour magazines for starlets and celebrities and pick out the ones that most appeal to you. Study how they wear their clothes. You will notice that they usually wear the clothes and the clothes don't wear them. See if you can come up with some looks like theirs on your own. Most shops have different versions of celebrity-type clothes at a fraction of the cost. You don't have to go bankrupt to look cool.

It's also good to keep in mind that your accessories can make or break your look. Knowing when to pare down on the bling and when to go all-out is crucial. Just take a cue from current fashionistas and see what they're doing. While it's never a good idea to wear multiple necklaces if you're dressed down, wearing a great men's vintage watch could make you look even cooler. So, as far as accessories go, I say less is more unless you're going for a trendier look. And never spend too much on costume jewelry. Save your big bucks for the real thing like a pair of diamond studs, which look good with anything, even sweatpants.

Lastly, keep in mind that it's never a good idea to waste money, even on clothes. If you are thinking about buying something you're not sure you're going to wear, then it might be a good idea to leave it on the rack. This is because if you're not sure of it, then you'll probably never wear it.

When you're shopping, it's always a good idea to visualize how any piece you buy is going to fit into your wardrobe. Imagine what you can do with a cashmere sweater and how many ways you could wear it before you buy it. If you can only come up with one way, then it's a piece that will be folded nicely in a drawer and never worn. Only buy things that you love and will fit with your lifestyle. This means you have to start being a little pickier with your clothes and what you buy. However, being a little pickier means having the foresight to know when something will work for you and your lifestyle and when something won't. Also, it will keep your bank account happier and your closet less cluttered.

In the end, it's ultimately *how* you wear something rather than *what* you wear. It's about knowing your limits and wearing clothes that make you feel confident whilst you're wearing them. Also, never wear something you don't feel comfortable wearing, whether it's a too short skirt or a crazy patterned shirt or loud colors. Only wear clothes that make you feel good and you will find that you are wearing the clothes and they are certainly not wearing you.

Never Underestimate the Power of a Great Pair of Jeans

You know how you're always looking for that great pair of jeans? In order to be a hottie, it's not only pertinent that you find yourself a great pair of jeans, but you allow yourself to *wear* them as well.

Does that sound a little weird to you? Okay, let me explain. Having a great pair of jeans is all well and good, but until you are brave enough to wear them and flaunt what you have, they'll just be hidden away and out of sight, much like your self-esteem. Getting something great like a good pair of jeans means that not only have you scored the best, you are becoming the best. It's about allowing yourself to be who you really are—a hot, confident woman—and not giving a damn about what anyone else thinks.

So to that I say, go out and find yourself exactly what you are looking for. In this chapter, I'll give tips on how to do just this. Keep in mind, that a great pair of jeans not only allows you to look good, but they can help you to feel good, too. Not only that, men love women in good jeans. Be prepared to attract them like crazy.

As women, we are all looking for the perfect pair of jeans. I know this to be a fact because I have been on this quest since what seems like the beginning of time. Because great jeans are so versatile, they are a staple in every woman's closet. They can take you from day to night without skipping a beat. With the perfect pair of jeans, you can wear them when you're out and about looking for a great deal shopping or you can pair them with a great top and some cute heels and hit the town. Also, a great pair of jeans not only makes you look good, but they make you feel good about yourself, too. This is why it is so important that you find yourself the perfect pair of jeans.

When looking for a great pair of jeans, it's all about the fit. When you try them on, be sure to bend down and sit and move around a little to get the feel of the jeans. It's essential that they also be comfortable, so jeans with a little stretch, as opposed to being one-hundred percent cotton, are what you're after. To put it another way: If you can't boogie-down in your jeans, then they're not the right pair for you.

To me, the rinse of the jeans isn't that important, but it might be a good idea to have several pairs in all different rinses—faded, dark, etc. Also, a little tattering looks good as long as the tattering doesn't go too far and looks ridiculous. I recently saw a young woman who was wearing a pair of tattered jeans that were what I would call over-tattered. They were tattered almost everywhere, even at the crotch. This isn't a good thing. Minimal tattering is best.

Additionally, having different cuts of jeans is also a good idea, too. Skinny jeans can really make a top—like a tunic—look great, while bootcut can really showcase your bottom. However, I suggest staying away from high-waisted jeans mainly because most of us aren't skinny enough to pull them off and, even then, they can tread too closely into "mom jeans" territory. And, if you're not careful, they will give you front-butt. This is something you don't want. Believe me, the mom jean look doesn't even look good on moms, so it's best to stay away from it if you possibly can. And the front-butt look? I don't think I need to qualify that one.

So what does getting a great pair of jeans have to do with being a hottie? It's about confidence, as I have said and will say throughout this book. I believe you should do whatever you can to give yourself more confidence. If that includes getting a great pair of jeans, then that's what it includes. Anything to give yourself more confidence is something worth doing.

When you are shopping for great jeans, it's not necessary to spend loads of money. I've found really great jeans in the lower range that work well with everything. If you want to go higher-end, just keep in mind that they will probably wear about like the less expensive kind. With jeans, the price point isn't the priority. What's important is that they fit well, you can move easily in them and they make you look good.

Having a great pair of jeans—or even a few great pairs—at your disposal will allow you to have more versatility with your wardrobe. You can pair great tops with jeans and sweaters and tunics. Jeans pretty much go with everything, so never underestimate the power of a great pair of jeans.

Keep in mind that if you find the perfect pair, my suggestion is to buy another pair exactly like your perfect ones so you can enjoy them for years to come. One last important note however regarding this: You need to try on every single pair of jeans before you buy. Even if they are the same brand, the same size, the same everything. No two pairs fit alike. I have found this to be true when, about two years ago, I came across the perfect pair of jeans. I wore them a few times a week before deciding I needed another reserve pair. After I got the reserve pair, I immediately threw them into the wash because I thought they'd fit just like my other pair. Wrong. They didn't and while they were still great jeans, the fabric was a little stiff. It was like they were a completely different kind of jean. What happened? All I can ascertain is that they were made at a different factory. But the fact of the matter is that jeans are usually unique. This is why you always have to try them on.

So, just keep in mind that almost no two pairs of jeans fit the same way. Try them on and don't waste your money on a sub-par pair. Also remember that finding the perfect pair means many days—and nights—of feeling more confident and sexier. And that's really the importance of a great pair of jeans.

One Good Bag

As with the chapter on a great pair of jeans, a great bag is yet another way to feel good about yourself. Knowing you have something really fabulous and that you're worth *having* something so fabulous can and will boost your confidence.

Most women love handbags. You may or may not feel the same but one way to really make yourself not only look better but feel better too is to get a really good bag.

And by "good bag," I mean one of high quality leather that is timeless and goes with everything. It should be a bag that you would be proud to carry on your arm. Keep in mind that this isn't necessarily about spending loads of money, but finding the perfect bag that fits your lifestyle. It's about style and higher quality stuff is always better in the long run, simply because it won't wear out over a year and is something you can keep forever and, quite possibly, hand down to your daughter.

One reason for having a great bag like this is that no matter what you're wearing, you will always look great. Say, for instance, you're just going out to the grocery store in a pair of cute sweats and flip-flops. If you have the addition of a great bag, you will still look like a million bucks. You will look like someone who knows about quality. And you'll make an impression. But, not only that, you will look like someone who *is* someone. I don't know why this is, but it's true. A great bag doesn't necessarily make you, but it makes *you* feel *good*. And that will give you a little bit more confidence. Or a lot. And having confidence is one of the most important things to being a hottie.

Now I know most men don't care what kind of bag you carry, and they really shouldn't, but those that know good bags will take note of you. And even if they don't know the designer, almost anyone can tell quality. And something will flash inside their minds: *This might be a girl who is worth getting to know better.*

Therefore, it is my advice to you to find yourself a really good bag. If the thought of spending some money on one makes you roll your eyes, don't worry. You can find used authentic designer goods in consignment shops and most all designers put their bags on sale a few times a year.

What to do is start saving for a great bag and when you come across it, you'll already have the money. (And, if you're like most women I know, you already have your eye on the purse of your dreams.) Just put a few dollars away each week into a "bag fund." Once it gets to the amount you are willing to spend, go out and look for what you want. Always look for quality, too. Notice the riveting and the stitching. Also, look for bags that have a vintage feel as those can make any outfit more appealing.

Other than making you look like a million bucks, a great bag can also make you feel like a million bucks. This is because knowing you care enough about yourself to buy something like this gives you a boost of confidence. And, as we all know, confidence is that we are after. Having confidence means having self-esteem and a girl with lots of self-esteem is a girl who will attract men like crazy.

Also note that *less is more* when buying bags. And by that I mean, it is never a good idea to waste your money on many inexpensive bags that you'll ultimately tire of. You should concentrate on buying fewer higher quality bags that you will keep a lifetime. Or, at the very least, a few years. And, if you do tire of them, you can usually sell them online for a good price.

The point is, when you buy a really great bag, you keep it. And when you concentrate on buying only quality bags, your closet won't be cluttered with bags that you regret buying. (If you're looking for something to do with all your old bags that you no longer want, most consignment shops take used bags, so you might want to check with them. Once you sell them, just put that money into your bag fund and you'll be closer to the bag of your dreams.)

Note: I am not telling you to purchase a bag on credit. You should never go in debt for a purse because that would sort of defeat the purpose. If you have to go into debt for it, the worry you will get from having to pay the bill will far outweigh any self-confidence you get from the bag. Instead, just save for the bag of your dreams. The gist here is to spend more on a bag, but buy fewer bags. Once you get a great bag, there won't be a need for another for a very long time. Monetarily, you should come out ahead in the long run with fewer purchases. Plus, your money will have gone for something of value.

On the other hand, if bags aren't your thing and you don't care about them, just get a good leather one in a neutral color—black leather *always* looks good. This can be your workhorse, your go-to everyday bag that goes with most everything in your wardrobe. You can find really great bags at outlet stores and on the internet or in your favorite department stores.

In the end, it doesn't really matter how much money you spend as long as you get something that will go with what you're wearing. Hotties always look good and they know the first step in looking good is having a great purse on their arm. Having a great bag gives you assurance in knowing you have not only the confidence and self-sufficiency to buy quality items, but you also have the wherewithal to pull together any outfit and look like a million bucks. So, look for a bag that you can use for everything and use it during the day, then maybe look for something smaller—like a clutch— that you can use for evening. And you can get a great clutch without breaking the bank, even if it's high-end designer. Also, you can sometimes find vintage alligator clutches, like the ones favored by Hollywood stars in the early years, at thrift stores and online for next to nothing. And vintage alligator in anything always looks good.

I know some might read this and wonder what getting a great bag has to do with being a desirable person and I say everything. What you're going for is a total look and leaving off an important detail such as the right bag means skimping on the look. While being a hottie isn't all about looks, it does pay to look your best at all times. And, with the right bag, even when you look not so great, you'll still look better than most.

Elegantly Tousled

One thing that separates hotties from the horde is the fact that they are usually elegantly tousled. Some might use the word disheveled instead of tousled, but when I think of disheveled, I get a vision of an old man stumbling around an alley holding onto a bottle wrapped in a paper sack. But when I think of tousled, I think of Brigitte Bardot—hot, sexy relaxed and always so feminine. She was the ultimate hottie and no one ever called her on her tousled hair.

Whether she's a brunette or a blonde or a redhead, a hottie is exactly like Brigitte Bardot. She is sexy, confident and elegantly tousled. She may or may not be French but, she is definitely sensuous. And she gets that sensuality by appearing to not really care about how she looks. Sure, she puts on her little bit of makeup and runs her hands through her hair and dresses in a sexy outfit, but she doesn't take too much effort. If her shirt is hanging a little out of the top of her skirt or her hair keeps falling into her eyes, she just continues on without giving it too much thought.

A hottie looks good without trying. That is the gist of it. She does this by being herself. No matter what she's wearing or how her hair looks, she still looks good. Hotties take care with their appearance but aren't prim and proper. They aren't stiff. They attract men because they look like they're out and about having a good time but aren't so uptight—and so meticulously dressed—that they seem unapproachable.

The "elegantly" part simply means that you care about what kind of clothes you wear but you have the appearance that you just threw together a great looking outfit. It means having manicured nails and a great pair of jeans on with a great t-shirt or sweater you picked up at a thrift store years ago. You pair that with a great pair of earrings or a vintage watch and you achieve the elegantly tousled look.

Another way of visualizing this is to say that you're not all matchy-matchy. Your outfit consists of a look that appears to be thrown together but was actually well thought out. And once you get the hang of it, you will graduate to being able to effortlessly accomplish this. Another good way to describe this would be to say that your high-end look meets bohemian chic. And that's a look that is completely and totally irresistible.

But it's not all about your clothes. Most of it is in your attitude.

To become elegantly tousled all you need to do is adopt an attitude of being sexy yet approachable. This entails acting like you just don't care. If some guy approaches you and wants to ask you out for a date, then fine, cool. If he doesn't? Fine, who cares? Being relaxed like this will not only make you feel better about yourself as a whole, but will enable you to attract more men. A woman who looks great but is obviously at ease with herself—hence the elegantly tousled look—is a woman a man wants to get to know better. And that's because you will look like you're a lot of fun to be around. You will look like someone who would carry a vintage Chanel bag but would also eat a hotdog from a street vendor. In essence, you have style and class but you also have an independent streak. You are always your own person and by own person, I do not mean you're the kind of girl who hangs from chandeliers during a wild night of partying, but one who wouldn't mind attending a football game or going to a laid-back barbeque with beers and pork. You're comfortable with your surroundings and as well as in your clothes. If you can manage to pull this off, you will be the girl that every guy wants. Not only will you be a girl who is desired by men, you'll be the girl who's also cool to hang out with. And that's what all men want. They want a woman who looks great, is at ease with herself and her surroundings but also doesn't mind throwing back a few beers.

With this in mind, know that what you are doing is not changing who you are but changing the false impression you may be giving off to the world. Most people are unaware of how they're being perceived. It's important to gain control of that. A lot of people come off as stiff and unapproachable when in reality they are not. This is what you're working on.

Men are attracted to women that they feel they can approach without being rejected. So, wouldn't it make sense that if you look sexy, yet casual, a man would feel more comfortable approaching you? Of course it would.

So, the thing to do when you go out is just relax. Put together a great outfit but make sure you don't look like you're on your way to work—or a conference or a funeral. Be more free-flowing and at ease not only with yourself but your wardrobe as well. And this will attract men like crazy.

Hottie Secret Alert

Another thing that separates hotties from the rest of the pack is the fact that hotties know their importance. In fact, they know their worth and value as a woman. Because of this, they have adopted an attitude of knowing that it's okay if a guy makes a big deal over them. It's okay if he insists on opening the car door for them. In fact, it's not only okay, it's expected.

To be a desirable person, you must adopt an attitude of not only knowing but also asserting your importance around men. And when I say this, I do not mean that you act like a bitch if he forgets to bring flowers or make a big deal over you. What I mean is that you know your worth and aren't afraid to let other people know it as well.

People treat you how you treat yourself. So, if you treat yourself like it's okay to be overlooked, then most likely, you will be. Some people will say that this is gracious behavior on your part and that you're just showing that you're above such pettiness. But it's not really. Other people will say that you're just showing that you're confident, but this isn't showing confidence. At least not when it comes to a relationship. In a relationship, you have to assert your value if it is not recognized. You can pretend that it's okay to be ignored by a complete stranger but with a guy you're going out with? Never. When you do this in a relationship, this is showing timidity and reluctance over not totally accepting your value. And if you don't accept it and expect good treatment for it, then no one else, particularly men, will either.

A good way to assert your importance, and this is always a good idea when involved in a relationship, is to never be afraid of who you are. It means never shrinking into the background. Whoever you go, you are at home and you are comfortable. And this is because you are comfortable in your own skin. This means you belong. I can't emphasize this point enough. Feeling like you are somebody means that you *are* somebody. If, however, you don't feel like somebody, then you're going to be treated like a nobody. It's that simple. And this doesn't mean you have to put on airs or pretend to be someone other than who you truly are. No. It means that you just love and respect yourself enough to act like you deserve to be treated well wherever you go or with whomever you go with.

So, don't be afraid to expect to be treated well. Don't be afraid to call him out if he's ignoring you. You have value and worth and if some guy isn't willing to give it to you? Such treatment is grounds for termination. Bye-bye, jerk.

Just a little reiteration: Know your value. Know your importance. Know you are worth something because you are. And never let anyone tell you otherwise. If they do, that means they're not worth knowing.

Flirty, Nice and Only Slightly Interested

Want to drive men crazy? Then act like this: Flirty, nice and only *slightly* interested.

This means that when you meet a guy you'd love to date, you don't let him know that you're interested. You keep it to yourself. But—and here's the rub—you let him know that he *might* stand a chance. Maybe. And you do this by being nice, a little flirty but only slightly interested.

Doing this will drive him crazy. He wants to know if you like him, but if he's unsure, then he usually won't stop until he finds out. And if he outright asks you? Just tell him, "Um, I'm not sure what you're insinuating. But, yeah, we could hang out sometime maybe."

This ambiguity drives men wild. While they do want a definite answer on what you're feeling for them, keep in mind that the more you hold back, the more interested they will get. This can be tough, especially of you really like a guy. So, the trick is to not give yourself away and just play it cool. And it's always advantageous to use this particularly male character trait to your advantage. And the trait we're talking about? His natural curiosity, of course. Keep in mind that men like to definitely know things. They don't like to guess. When you keep them guessing, you risk driving them crazy. And that means they become more and more interested to figure you out.

A desirable woman is usually never aggressive with a man because she doesn't have to be. She knows that sooner or later one is going to show up and want to date her. She isn't worrying about coming across as a bitch or about scaring any man away. She's just herself and is naturally relaxed and at ease. In essence, to be a desirable woman means to be your own person and set your own pace. If a man is interested in her, that's fine and if he isn't, that's fine too. She's not waiting on him to make her world better because her world is already pretty darn good and if he can add to her enjoyment with his company? Then all the better. This means she acts like she just doesn't care. And really, how hard is that to do? The best thing about this? It always works. The less a hottie seems to care about some guy, the more he seems to care about her. Funny how that works.

Now while you're only going to act slightly interested, do yourself a favor and really listen to what he's saying. This may sound like a bit of a contradiction but it isn't. While you're going to hold back how you feel for him, make sure he knows you're interested in what he's saying. This is a huge ego boost for most men and by doing this you're showing him you care about his opinion. Of course, this doesn't mean to hang on every word, but just listen to what he's saying.

Therefore, whenever you're talking to a guy, learn how to listen. Guys love it when women take the time to really pay attention to what they are saying and to ask questions about their lives. Obviously, you don't have to talk his ear off, and you shouldn't want to. Just ease into the conversation and ask him questions about himself while you're answering his questions about you. While you're talking, if his attention goes a little flat, I'd suggest excusing yourself for a while. Go get yourself a drink or maybe just go the ladies room and touch up your makeup. However, don't stay gone too long. Just about ten minutes or so, just long enough for him to know that you're not at his beck and call. This will remind him that he's not the only game in town and if he wants to know you better, he might want to straighten up and put his attention back on you. If you come back and his attention is still divided between you and, say, the wall? Tell him it was nice talking to him but you have to get up early the next morning. And say goodnight. It's just my opinion that men who act like this right off the bat aren't going to get any better on down the road. It's best not to be rude and simply play it cool, like you're oblivious to his odd behavior.

Keep in mind that this approach works well in a club situation but not if you're out to dinner. If you're out to dinner or whatever with him and this happens, it might just be best to just hang out until the evening ends, and then see how it plays out. If he doesn't call you after the date? Then that's his loss. There's no sense on trying too hard for some guy who's not that interested. When men do this, it's obvious that they're not that interested. So, say goodbye and find someone who is *that* interested.

Women who are wanted and desired aren't content to rest on their laurels. They would never hang around a guy who wasn't that interested in them. If you have the confidence to be done with a conversation or a guy who doesn't seem to really want to get to know you better, then you are a true hottie. Chances are, if you do this, he'll come running after you once you've struck up a conversation with another man. Then it's up to you to decide if he's worth your time. And that will be your call.

Men are the natural aggressors, we can all agree on that. However, being confident in yourself means that you are in control. Hotties are desired and get what they want. So, don't be shy about losing a loser when he becomes disinterested. If you can learn to do this without so much as a second thought, you will have men eating out of your hand and that's because you're showing them that, while they might be not be that interested right now, you're certainly not desperate enough to hang around until they are.

Keep in mind that you need to be sure not to play it *too* cool with someone you really like; otherwise, it might drive him off. A balance must be achieved. You do this by throwing him a bone every once in a while or you might find yourself by yourself. Just play it cool but never cold. This means to never snub him or make fun of him in any way. Pay him due respect just don't fall all over him and tell him he's the greatest thing since sliced bread. Be flirty, nice and only slightly interested. And you'll probably win him over.

Marriage Isn't the Goal

Marriage isn't the goal when it comes to dating. Mostly, dating is a lot like interviewing for different jobs. Say, for instance, you just graduated college with a highly desirable degree and you have all kinds of job offers. Right? Everyone wants a piece of you. You've got that big degree and all kinds of companies need someone like you to come in and help them out. When you're in this sort of position, you're not going to take the first job offered; that would be a waste of all those hard years you spent toiling over the books. You're going to feel things out a little and see just what all's out there in the world for you and figure out what place is the best fit. You gather your information and then get the best job with the best pay you possibly can.

Shouldn't you do that while dating, as well? I think you should.

That's why marriage, like a good job offer, is a goal but isn't the end-all-be-all. Marriage is fine when it comes along. But in the meanwhile, you're a free spirit and that means when you find the man you want, then you can marry him. Until then, just have fun.

Again, it's the relaxed attitude that must prevail. If you can't relax enough to allow men to come to you, then you might become or be seen as a little desperate and a little desperate can only mean one thing: You are blocking whatever good men that might come into your life by being too eager.

That's right. If you find that you are desperate to get married because your mom is pressuring you or you're getting older or whatever, then you're forcing the issue. And, let me tell you, forcing the issue of marriage with any man is a bad idea. Why? Because it will make them run. Men seem to be naturally opposed to getting married these days anyway. Who knows why or even cares? This means that you should not sit around and wait for a man to come into your life in order to make it complete. It means that your life, right now, is pretty damn good and whatever man comes in will only enhance it, not make it.

This sort of attitude will really land you a lot of men, some of which will probably want to marry you. Men want to marry women that aren't desperate to get married. So, by showing any sort of desperation on this subject, you can probably expect him to hit the bricks. This is why you should never act desperate to get married or go on a date or to move in or whatever. It's important that men think that these things are their ideas. It's best to set marriage aside right now and just be a confident and desirable person. Then you can have your choice of men to marry.

But what if marriage is your goal? What if this is what you really want? There are women who really want to get married and you can't judge them for it. There's nothing wrong with it, after all and it's a great goal to have. To these women I would suggest cooling it a little with the marriage thing. First things first—get the man and then work on marriage. It may come in time, but right now just enjoy being single and in the game. And once guys begin to pick up on this from you, then they will want to hang around you more and more.

You should also understand that there will be men you run across whose goal *is* marriage. Just like some women, there are men who want nothing more than to tie the knot. If this is your goal and you run across a desirable guy like this, then you're one lucky lady and you can probably start talking about it right off the bat. Since this is not always going to be the case, it might be better, however, to just wait until he brings it up. And if it's his goal, he will, believe me. There are many people out there who want marriage and, hey, why not? It's part of life and should be a goal. Nothing is wrong with that. But it's just best, at first, to take it easy on the "M" word, unless, of course, he brings it up first.

Milk for Free?

It might be worth mentioning that it's never good to give *it* away too quickly or too easily. Milk, I mean. Okay, if you've never heard the saying, I will say it here: "Why should he pay for the cow when he's getting the milk for free?" This means why should he marry you if you're already giving him sex?

I have mixed feelings about this statement. I agree with it and I don't agree with it at the same time. I don't think anyone should keep themselves pure and chaste just to land a man. I also think sex between two consulting adults shouldn't have any sort of negative connotations. However, I do know that men view sex differently than women do. And I do know that men can become a little complacent in a relationship and not want to pay for the milk once he starts getting it for free on a regular basis.

What to do? What to do?

The thing is if you are in a committed, adult relationship, you're probably going to be having sex frequently as this is probably the best thing about *being* in a new relationship. Sex is good. It's fun. Why not? And I am sure your guy will feel the same way, too. With sex being enjoyed by both partners, it's hard to play games with it, no pun intended. Especially if you're already in the relationship. But what about before you land a man and get into a committed relationship? What about the milk then? What should you *do* with the milk? Well, and this is just my opinion, if you want to sleep around, that's your choice. But if you do, keep in mind that many men think a woman who sleeps around too much or too soon into the relationship won't make good marriage material. Don't ask me why, as we all know they want to sleep with as many women as possible, but that's the way some men think. Maybe it's because they have low self-esteem and think that if someone sleeps with them too easily then she really must have low standards. Who knows? It's a double-standard that isn't going away anytime soon.

Personally, I don't think women should have to be chaste and virginal. That's not what it's about. But it is about using some restraint and some common sense when it comes to sex. Use your best judgment with any situation and if you're only sleeping with the guy for fun, then that's what it is and make the most of it. However, if you find a guy that you think might be marriage material, maybe hold out on him a little and see where it goes. It's my opinion that it's never a good idea to hop into bed with just anyone but it's especially not a good idea to hop into bed with a guy that you might see as being your future husband. With a case like this, it's best to hold out and see where the relationship goes before bringing sex into the equation.

I know that some women do have sex with a lot of guys and it's usually not out of desire, either. They get desperate and sleep with just about anyone in order to get them to like them. You do not have to do this! He will either like you or not, with or without sex. If he only wants to sleep with you, that means he doesn't want a relationship. It's the men you run across who want to get to know you better, regardless of whether you sleep with them or not, that are worth spending time with.

Granted, the goal for many men is, more or less, to get sex from whatever woman they're interested in at that time. If you prolong the sex, this will make the relationship more intense and more special. Just keep in mind that if you just give it away on the first date, he's probably not going to want to be more than bed buddies. Now, there are some men that won't mind this, of course, and will count themselves as lucky that a hot woman like you would sleep with them so soon. However, that man is a rarity and if you find someone special that you could really see yourself with, then it's best to hold off for a little while until you've secured his interest. Men can and do lose interest after they've bedded a woman and a woman who doesn't hop into the sack right off the bat is a woman with mystery and a little mystery can really pump up the interest.

Plastic Surgery?

While I am not a person to advocate plastic surgery, I do understand the allure and I do understand that there are some out there who may have things they want to "fix." It's not up to me, or anyone else for that matter, to judge. I don't condemn nor do I condone. And here's why.

I know this young woman who hated her nose. And by hate I mean she *loathed* her nose. She would lament about how it made her feel "ugly" and "undesirable." When she looked at herself in the mirror, it was the only thing about her face that she saw and she saw a flaw she couldn't get past. When she turned eighteen years old, she was lucky enough that her mother agreed to pay for a nose job. When I heard about it, I just sort of rolled my eyes, thinking it wasn't going to change the way she felt about herself. But I was wrong. It did change the way she viewed herself and after the bandages came off, she had more confidence, would smile more and was generally happier. Could she have gone to a psychologist first so that she could have overcome this self-image problem? I don't know. As far as I know, that was never an option for her. She never even considered it. She just wanted her nose "fixed." End of story.

Again, I don't condone nor condemn plastic surgery. I am merely relating what I know. So, before you make an appointment to fix whatever you feel is "wrong" with you, try to learn to love your "flaws." Remember what you see as flaws, other people might love because they are part of you and help make you who you are. Part of being a person who is desired is accepting and loving yourself for yourself. That's the groundwork you will lay in order to fully come into being the great person you are.

I think what it boils down to is this: If you go into something like plastic surgery with the right attitude, it can be good. If you know it's only going to fix something cosmetic and don't expect it to turn your life completely around, then it's fine. I do know people who've had nose jobs, boob jobs and liposuction all with great results. If you do decide to go under the knife, you really need to think about why you want work done. How will it improve your life? Will it make you look better, feel better or just act better?

Don't ever go into something as dangerous as surgery easily. And with plastic surgery, less is more, literally. You don't want to go out and overhaul your whole body, as we've seen some celebrities do. No, no, no. You only want to enhance what you have, not change it completely. A nose or boob job is one thing. A total Frankenstein-ish do-over is just plain creepy. And, let's face it, it does make you look plastic. (They don't call it *plastic* surgery for nothing.)

Therefore, I think it is necessary for anyone who thinks that a little tweak here or there will improve their lives to sit back and figure out why they want do it. To do it or not to do it is totally in your hands and don't let anyone else— mother, boyfriend, etc.—decide for you. We all know men love big boobs, but it's not the guy that's going to go through all that pain to get them. And, yes, having plastic surgery is very painful. That's something else to consider while making your decision.

So, decide for yourself if this is something that you think will truly benefit you. If you decide to do it, it is imperative that you get a board-certified plastic surgeon to do the work. And by that I mean, look them up, do research and get referrals. There are a lot of these people who do surgeries that aren't even doctors or they specialize in someone else entirely like dentistry or podiatry. You don't want to get butchered and become a statistic. This is not a decision to be taken lightly.

Keep in mind that being a hottie isn't about being perfect. It's about being perfectly you. That's what you're after and if you can get to that state of mind, I doubt you'll ever need plastic surgery to boost your confidence.

To Botox or Not to Botox?

All of us women will probably eventually get to that point in our lives where we may start to panic about wrinkles. It can be a hard thing to deal with when the lines start appearing and you begin to look older. We try wrinkle creams and exfoliants and do just about everything to avoid those dastardly things. But there is no avoiding them. They happen. And while they may give men "character," we tend to feel like they just make us look old.

But don't be like that.

I think we should embrace our wrinkles. We've most likely earned them, right? As women, we've had to put up with a lot—a lot of bad boyfriends, husbands, glass ceilings, crazy families, etc. You name it, there's probably a reason for the wrinkles. And, whatever it is, we've earned them.

But what if we don't want to look like we've earned any of them? What if we want to look like we've lived lives of leisure? What do we do then? Since the advent of Botox we now have a choice—wrinkled or wrinkle free? It's now a part of our culture. It's the thing movie stars and housewives alike end up doing. But should we?

As with plastic surgery, I don't condemn nor condone Botox. In fact, I don't see anything wrong with it. However, if you go overboard with it, you can and will look a little freakish. So, if Botox is something that you want to do, because there are risks involved, just make sure that an actual doctor, as in a M.D., does the actual injecting. Also keep in mind that if you do get it, your face might look a little frozen. I know someone who got Botox injections and it was hard to look at her because it appeared that her face had been frozen into an expression of surprise. Whatever you said to her, you would momentarily think you had startled her or that she was shocked at what you just said. If you told her something as mundane as you'd just washed your car, she'd look surprised even though she wasn't. It was a little disconcerting, to say the least.

So, to Botox or not to Botox? As with anything, moderation is the key and it's a personal decision. And take it with a grain of salt. Don't think that it will change your life because it won't. It will just get rid of your wrinkles. While being a hottie is about looking good, it's mostly in your attitude. So, just by adjusting your attitude a little, you might find that you don't need or want Botox. Men, at least men worth dating, don't really seem to care that much one way or another. But this isn't about men or pleasing men. It's about women wanting to look their best. And I am all for that. But just use caution. Botox is a highly toxic chemical and can cause serious damage if you're allergic to it. Be sure to consult with a qualified physician before you make your decision and ask about any side effects.

Shed Your Stuff

Becoming a hottie is more about shedding the old image of yourself than anything else. It's like taking off a mask and revealing the true you. Or, if you'd like to think of it another more corny way, it's like you're breaking out of your cocoon and spreading your wings to fly like a beautiful butterfly. While this does sound silly, it is true.

But shedding this old image means that you should never be too tied to unimportant things in your past. This might mean old slights and insults that have been dealt to you, but it could also mean your stuff. Yes, your stuff and by this I mean all the junk that you've collected through the years. When you hold on too tightly to objects from the past, it can begin to start shaping your future if you're not careful. This is why you should never be tied to your possessions. I mean, what's the point? What if you get a great job offer overseas? That means you'll have a lot of stuff to sort through before you can hop that plane. So, it's best to keep your place fairly free of clutter and unwanted things. We all want to keep the jeans we wore in high school for some reason. Well, I never did, but I know people like this. If you are one of these people, it's time to get rid of all that old stuff and allow new stuff to enter into your life.

Now some people might read this and think, "What does tidying my place up have to do with being a hottie?" Well, quite a bit. If you aren't in control of your surroundings, how can you be in control of your life? If you can just imagine it for a moment, think about meeting a really great guy. Think about bringing him back to your place. Now think about how it's cluttered with unused furniture, magazines, etc... (If it is this way, I mean.) It might even be a little dirty. Now, if you want to get a little "dirty" with him, you need some room for that, right? And what if, God forbid, he wants to eventually move in with you? Does your closet warrant that kind of commitment?

Think about it. Do you want to attract men like crazy and eventually find one that you'd like to keep around? If the answer is yes, then it might be time to literally make room for him in your life. By doing this, you are opening yourself up to more. Thinking about having a man in your life and where would he fit is a great way to attract him on in. (This goes along with the Law of Attraction principals I used in my other book, *How to Be Wanted.*) Like I said, that's why shedding old stuff allows new stuff to enter in.

If your place is stuffed to the brim with—let's not mince words here, either—old junk, even if you are able to get some great new stuff, you'd have no room for it. De-cluttering is a sure fire way to help attract new things into your life and if the new thing you really want is a new man, then all the better. Make some room for that man!

Obviously, this isn't just for him, either. It's about you, too. There is something cathartic about shedding old stuff that really and truly makes you feel like a new person. Attacking an overstuffed closet and getting rid of half the junk in there is good soul work. While I know some won't agree, it does do you good.

Organizing will also help you find out what great things you already have in your life that you may have forgotten about. I have my grandfather's hat, which is probably close to sixty-years old. It was actually hidden under a bunch of old junk and when I accidently stumbled upon it, it really made me feel good. *That's where it was!* Something I really cared about was hidden under a bunch of stuff I could care less about.

See what I'm getting at? Shedding your stuff can help bring back old memories and give you a little more room in the meanwhile. And, let's face it, it can make you feel so good about yourself.

Being a hottie means being a woman who's in control of her life. If your home life is a little chaotic because of clutter, it's time to take back control. And it's easy, too. All you have to do is get in there and start pulling stuff out. Make piles of stuff—keep, sell and garbage. Keep only the best stuff you have, sell what you can—Ebay, consignment, etc.—and then throw the truly stained, spotted, ripped, torn and just plain ugly and useless in the garbage. (A good rule of thumb is to recycle as much as possible and only throw out what can't be salvaged in any way possible.)

Another good thing about doing this is that you might already have some really great clothes you've forgotten about. All the better! I go through my closet about twice a year and every time I do it, I find something I'd forgotten about and really like.

If you have a pile of clothes that you don't want to sell for some reason, call up all your girlfriends and have a clothes swap. All this entails is that each of you clean out your closets in the way described then bring all your "unwanted" stuff to someone's place, then you go through each other's things. And then you swap. Sally might want that yellow cashmere sweater you just couldn't get into but bought because you found it on sale at such a great price. And you might want Jane's stilettos that pinch her feet. See what I'm getting at here? In addition to helping each other out, this can make for a really fun evening, as well. And it's not that hard to organize or to carry through. Who wouldn't want to go shopping for free? Not many women I know.

Note: You can also do this for home goods such as cappuccino machines or beauty products or whatever you don't use or have no intention of using.

Once you are done with your closet—or closets—just go into every room in your place and clean it out. Clean out from under the beds, take the cushions off the couch—

which seems to be a receptacle for change—as well as every cabinet in your kitchen. Now, once all this is done, the rule is to clean as you go. As you clean out your closet, take a dust cloth and some all purpose cleaner and dust shelves, and so on and so forth. When you're done, admire your work and feel good about having a nice, clean place.

This may seem daunting, but it really is kind of fun once you get into it. Just take a day per room—or closet—and tackle it. When you feel the pride that I know you will feel when this is accomplished, you'll start wanting to clean out that medicine cabinet or garage or whatever. You will feel the power of organization and you will want to experience it in all aspects of your life.

Of course, this chapter might not apply to everyone, as some are self-proclaimed neat freaks, but even those of you who keep a lid on clutter and dirt in their places know that every once in a while, every home can use a little de-cluttering and cleaning. This doesn't mean, however, to become obsessive about it; just get a handle on it and keep your place presentable.

Once this is done, getting control of your life will be easier. Having a messy home can split your focus and keep you from concentrating on being the great person you already are. And you don't want anything to do that. Taking care of chores like this means leaving open plenty of space in your mind to get out there and start driving men crazy. And that's what it's all about.

If you take the time to make your home more inviting, you might just get to invite more people into it. Any room can be made tidy and luxurious if you only take the time to pay some attention to it. And, let's be serious, a kitchen sink full of dirty dishes is enough to make anyone a little crazy.

Be a Smart Cookie, Financially

In my opinion, being financially independent is crucial if you want to be a confident person. This should be everyone's goal and the best reason for doing this is because it leads to personal independence. If you're dependent on anyone—parents, boyfriend, husbands, etc.—then you're ultimately at their mercy. This is not a situation any smart woman would want to find herself in. I know many women can't leave terrible marriages because they never bothered to establish their own line of credit!

And this leads me to my next point. A woman should never go into a relationship thinking that a man is going to take care of her. Sure, he can pay for dinner, but do not expect him to pay your credit cards or your rent. Unless, of course, he's your sugar daddy and then, more power to you! Kidding aside, it's best to keep in mind that if you do expect someone to take care of you financially, then don't be surprised when you find yourself completely dependent.

That's not a fun thought at all, is it?

But how can you become financially independent? How can you avoid being at the mercy of other people financially? If at all possible, get a better job, save money and know that no matter what happens, you can take care of yourself. This attitude will take the desperation out of getting married or finding a relationship. And the thing is, once you do this, you will not only become financially independent, but you will also open yourself up to better relationships. This is because you're not looking for a breadwinner but for someone that will enhance your life rather than be the reason for which you live. This means you can have whatever sort of relationship you wish to have.

If you're not dependent on a man for money, then you will be free to make better choices. Sure, you'd like a big house but maybe you're attracted to a man who's an artist and doesn't make much money. Well, maybe you can make enough for both of you. Not only does this put you in control of your destiny, in a way, it allows you to really explore what sort of relationships will work best for you. Also it will open you up to relationships with great men who may have lesser means.

Of course it goes without saying, if you want to marry money, then that's your choice. I don't have any problem with that and my mother always used to tell me, "You can love a rich man just as easily as you can love a poor man." While this may be true, rich men sometimes do come with a hefty price tag. They might expect more out of you if you're living on their dime. You may have to earn your keep, so to speak. So, there are many different aspects to consider if you chose this route.

When I'm talking about financial independence, I am not saying that you should only concentrate on your career and making money. While that is a good thing, you should also have fun in your life. You have to have a balance. Work hard but don't forget to stop and smell the roses. Don't forget to relax and enjoy life. Also, don't give so much of yourself to a career that you make your life torturous, either. As I said earlier, don't forget to indulge in the lazy. However, don't forget to keep your eyes on the prize of financial independence.

It's crucial that you always think about your future, financial and otherwise. It's not about *living* in the future, of course, but planning for it never hurts. And it never hurts to be financially secure and that means taking the time now to be financially smart. This will help when you do get married, if that's what you want, of course, and if you have children. Being financially independent right now might make the difference of whether you can take more time off to be with your baby once it's born. And a good way to start is to get out of debt. That means, no more paying for dinner out with the girls on credit. Instead, ask everyone over and have a barbecue or spaghetti dinner. This means laying off the online shopping—I know many of us are too addicted to this—and instead save that money you would spend to help pay off existing debt. This means really learning how money works and working it to your advantage.

There are all kinds of ways to cut back on spending and to pay off existing debt but the easiest and most effective way is to just start. That's right, just start today. And all you have to do is gather all your bills, sit down with them, write them out, add them up and then subtract that money from what you actually bring home with your paycheck. Whatever is left over should go to pay off smaller credit card debt first, then onto the bigger ones until you have all them paid off. Then you can work on paying your car off. In the meanwhile, save as much as you can.

Of course, as you read this, you might be thinking about the chapters on buying a great bag or pair of jeans. You might be thinking that this goes against what I was saying earlier, but it really doesn't. When you buy these things, your goal should be always to *pay cash*. And not to the detriment of your personal finances. So while you're getting your financial situation straightened out, all you have to do is set aside some money with which to purchase these things. Of course, you don't even have to buy a bag or whatever if you don't want to. That was just a suggestion, but as you pay off debt, you will need to reward yourself in some way so it makes it worth your time and don't get discouraged. Therefore, your reward for doing this will be that great bag or pair of jeans or whatever. But do keep in mind that you should keep your purchases small until you pay off existing debt.

Let me reiterate: Don't buy anything if you have a mountain of debt until you pay that debt either off or way down. Only pay cash for a great bag or jeans or whatever. That is, if you can afford it.

Also, I'd be willing to bet that if you do have a lot of credit card debt that you've already got a pretty nice wardrobe. If you're one of those girls with an overflowing closet, as mentioned in the previous chapter, why not take this time to do a little inventory? And once you do that, why not see if you can sell some of your great stuff and take that money and either put it towards your bag or pay it on your bills? Especially if it's something that you don't wear.

Most women have been taught to wait for a knight in shining armor—or at the very least, a man with a really good paying job—who will ride up, sweep them off their feet, make love to them and then share his wealth. Oh, if that were only true! But it isn't. There is no knight and the idea of depending on some man to bankroll our lifestyles isn't really that appealing. Or it may be to some and if so, no judgments. To each their own. But if you err on the side of caution and you want to be able to always call the shots in your life, get some financial independence. It is the best way to ensure that if you are unfortunate enough to get into a bad relationship, you will be fortunate enough to get out of it, if need be.

Money should be fun, too. It should be fun to make it and to save it. And to spend it, as well. But actually paying for things with cash rather than getting them on credit is where the true satisfaction of buying things comes from. Paying cash for things will give you loads of confidence. It means you can earn your own money and pay your own way and that is, indeed, a very good feeling without the guilt that comes from a large credit card bill. It means that once you buy something, it's yours and you don't have to worry about paying for it later.

While money can solve a lot of problems, it can also be a big source of consternation. That's why it's always a good idea to make your own money so you get the say so in how it's spent and saved. Also, the worry over money is a real downer, so the better off you are, the better you will feel. Who wants to worry about covering the rent or mortgage? Make a plan to pay that sucker off and be financially free. That's the makings of a good life because once you have some financial independence, you will begin to experience more freedom and more freedom means less worry and less worry means more fun.

The best part of being financially independent is that you know that no matter what happens you can take care of yourself. It's knowing that you aren't dependent on a man or on your parents to see you through the tough times. This means no one can tell you want to do! And that is the best feeling possible.

So, try to attain this one goal. Try to become financially independent. When you do, you will feel so much self-empowerment that you'd be a fool to ever think about waiting for your knight in shining armor. Once you can attain this goal, you will feel more confidence and more comfortable in yourself. It is crucial to being a desirable person. And it takes a lot of worry away, too.

Get What You Want the First Time

Less is more. But having more isn't so bad. And what I mean by *more* is having better than average things. If you buy the best there is or the best that you can afford, you will be satisfied with what you've bought and you won't want to keep going out and buying even more. Say you want a designer belt that costs a few hundred dollars. Try as you may to justify this, you can't and you end up buying another lesser belt instead of the one you really want. And then you buy another one because that one wasn't the exact one you wanted. And then another and another. And then by the time you're done, you could have bought the more expensive one three or four times over.

Get what I'm saying?

Luxury is nice and when you save your money for things of luxury you will want less of the less luxurious stuff. You don't have to have ten designer purses—though that would be very, very nice—but having one is like having ten lesser bags that will just gather dust in your closet. See what I'm getting at? If you buy what you want the first time, you'll ultimately end up spending less money. This is because if you're not always chasing after something that is *sort* of like what you want or *kind* of like what you want or just as *good* as what you want, you're actually getting what you want the first time. And when you get what you want the first time, you don't have to worry about getting it any more.

And this isn't just about money. It's about a state of mind. And that's why only wanting a few, nicer things comes into play. If you just want one great bag or belt or whatever, that's a pretty easy thing to do. This means you will want less, but you will actually end up getting more.

The need for lots of stuff, as discussed, sometimes means we are merely trying to fill a hole in our lives. While I am all for getting what you want out of life, I think you should be diligent about what you want and that means not settling for less than what you want. This way, you get it and then once you do, you're not immediately pining for something else. So, less is more but more can actually be less.

Think of this when you are out and about shopping. Think about quality and not quantity. Get what you want but be willing to wait until you can afford it. In the meanwhile, make do with what you have. This is a sure-fire way to set yourself up nicely without killing your bank account or maxing out your credit cards.

It's About Being Stylish, Not Slutty

As they say, slutty is as slutty does. You don't want to be slutty. You want to be stylish but you still want to be sexy. If you can pull this off, you will be a hottie in no time flat.

Ideally, you should try to attract attention to who you are rather than what you're wearing. While your clothes should be stylish, others should see you, not the clothes. You should not attract attention by wearing outlandishly revealing outfits but by being yourself.

And that's a great thing to aspire to. You are who you are, in spite of what sort of clothes you are wearing. You don't have to be desperate to attract a man, but a man should be desperate to attract your attention. This is the main reason some women go overboard with the sexiness. But it's not really necessary. By simply changing your perspective, you will be more in control than ever before. And that's a great place to find yourself.

Now I am not a prude by any stretch of the imagination and I think it's great to dress sexily. However, there are limitations. If we lived in an ideal world, a woman would be able to wear whatever she wants without anyone batting an eye. But we don't. I know this sounds old-fashioned, but men can get the wrong idea about a girl if she dresses a little too provocatively and won't give her due respect. I, personally, think this is ridiculous. Why should it matter how you dress? Why should the way you dress have any bearing on what others think about you? I don't know the answers to those questions; I just know that it does matter.

I just want to take a few minutes here to go over something. Many people equate being a hottie with being a slut and that's just not the case. Being a hottie is so much more than that. Being a hottie is being confident, sexy and knowing that you deserve respect. So, when you are thinking of how to style yourself, think about actual style before you think about sexiness. Too much of anything just won't work. And by that I mean, too much cleavage, too much butt, too much jewelry, too much leg, etc.

Looking your best can be looked at as being a style choice, of course, and what you wear can make or break you in this regard. So, be diligent in your choice of clothes. You don't want to look like you're walking the street when you go out at night. You want to look classic, stylish and hip, but not slutty.

Yes, looking slutty and wearing revealing clothes will attract the attention of men. Why wouldn't it? But what kind of guys are you attracting? I mean, seriously, think about that. You want to attract guys who are actually interested in talking to—and perhaps even dating—you, not just sleeping with you. So, by keeping your clothes on the less revealing side, you are making sure you aren't attracting the wrong element. Keep in mind that you don't want to cast your net too wide because you can and will catch too many fish and most of them you will want to throw back. This is the main problem with dressing too sexy.

This brings me to my next point, which is about being desperate. I think that many women dress in revealing clothes because they are desperate for attention. And I also think this is the wrong way to go about it because you probably won't attract the "right "kind of attention. Sure, that might make me sound old-fashioned but I am a true believer in quality not quantity. So, by putting your goods on the market like that, you're basically telling men that you're easy and a little desperate. Hotties are not easy or slutty. And they're certainly not desperate.

While it's good to express sexuality and there is nothing, in my personal opinion, wrong with wearing sexy clothes in and of itself, the problem lies in that it can give some guys the wrong idea. And then they think they have the green light to do and say anything to you. You do not want this. Why put up with these jerks? It's best to keep a check on this and wear sexy things that aren't too revealing. That way, you don't look desperate and you actually attract men with intelligence who aren't just out looking to get laid, but are out looking for love.

Fashionistas of the Past

If you want to get an idea of how to throw together great looks or how to really be a hottie that men will flock to, take a cue from some of the legends of the past. You can do this by watching classic movies.

The all-time favorite for many women is, of course, *Breakfast at Tiffany's* starring Audrey Hepburn. I don't think I need to spend too much time talking about this one as almost every woman I know has seen it and loved it and devoured it. However, it wouldn't hurt to take a refresher course and watch it again. When you are watching it, really look at how it's filmed. Study the acting and clothes. While these movies may not reflect your own personal style or portray someone you'd want to aspire to be like, watching classic movies like this will get you in the mind-frame of what it's like to be desired and wanted. Getting that feeling of desirability will allow you to recognize it once it happens to you. Of course, I am sure you've already experienced this feeling many times over, but it never hurts to get a different perspective on it. Besides, it's a good movie.

Another great movie is *Darling* starring Julie Christie, which is one of my all-time favorites. While the character doesn't end up with her fairy-tale ending, she has a great time getting to the end and she looks so stylish! It's a movie that you can really sink your teeth into and, not only that, it makes you think.

Additionally, it's always a good idea to be well-read and one way to get some fantastic inspiration is to read books written about the legends of screen and fashion. Books on silent film actresses or stars from the forties are also great. These women really had that "it" factor and they used it.

There was just so much more glamour back then. Reading books like this will help to motivate you.

Another great source of inspiration is books on fashion legends like Coco Chanel as well as the famous fashion editor, Diana Vreeland. These can give you inspiration to know what it's like to start from the bottom and work your way to the top. Coco Chanel is a favorite amongst most women, mainly because she was just so damn fabulous. Chanel was a hottie in her own time because she did things her own way. And that's what you should do, do things your own way. Find your way and you will find that you are more than fabulous. Allow yourself to be fabulous and allow your self-esteem to rise. You are you for a reason and that means you can be as fabulous as you like. So, read up on confident women of the past. Find women you admire and read their biographies

You can also be inspired by documentaries on artists and fashion. Just find what most interests you and Google it and then do your research. It's not only educational and inspirational, it's really a lot of fun, too.

The point of all of this is inspiration and with inspiration comes motivation. And when these two important factors prevail, that makes for one fabulous hottie.

Hottie Haters

Seriously. When you are a hottie, you're going to get a lot of haters. This is because some women tend to be a bit jealous of confident women. I wish it weren't so, but it is. So, when you become the hottie you were meant to become, get ready for a bit of backlash, but do not let it deter you. If you know what you're up against, then you will prevail.

Let me tell you the story of a hottie hater. A few years ago, I was out to lunch with a good friend. And while this friend is a bit of a downer, I do like her and wanted to spend some time catching up with her because she'd been living out of the country for a while. After we were seated, we got into our usual talk of "how's it going" and "what have you been up to?" and all that. Shortly thereafter, a group of people entered the restaurant and within this group was a pretty young woman wearing a very nice business-type outfit. I thought she looked good but didn't give her much more thought than that. Well, my friend, who is, regrettably, well-equipped at putting others down, basically went off on this girl. She said, "Look at her! Where does she think she is?" She then started laughing. "Doesn't she realize she's at Joe's?" (Joe's is basically a family-style bar and grill.) I just sat there not knowing what to think. Was my friend serious? Was she seriously putting this well-dressed young woman down? And for what? Because she opted to throw on a nice outfit and not the normal jeans and t-shirt look that is so typical of Joe's? It was really kind of disturbing.

This revealed more about my friend than the girl obviously.

My friend was a hottie hater. It wasn't until a few years later that I looked back at this incident and realized what she was doing. I didn't get it then because I am not like that. I don't ever think it's a good idea to make fun of anyone for any reason. (I'm a big believer in karma.) But that's what she was doing. She was putting this woman down because she looked better than she did. She was jealous and because this girl was dressed nice and looked good, she wanted to turn the girl's strength into a weakness. She wanted to make the fact that she was a hottie into something bad and inappropriate. My friend was (and still is) a hottie hater and it showed. And you know what? It didn't make me think any less of the other woman, but it did make me think less of my friend. Who was she to do this to that woman? It was nothing more than her showing her low self-esteem.

So, just keep in mind that when you start strutting your stuff, you may get a little backlash. But, like I said, don't let it deter you! Just keep on truckin' as they say. And be aware of the hottie haters, who usually come in the form of someone who doesn't look quite as good as you. You should keep in mind that many women are insecure and territorial and get very displeased if anyone makes an effort to look good and act confident. It makes them feel *less than* and the only way they think that they can regain the superiority they think they have is to put down the people who are more put together than them. If they would just make an effort on their own part to improve themselves so they didn't feel inferior, it would make life much, much easier for everyone else.

Therefore, when you come across a hottie hater, you just have to realize that for some reason, something about you threatens them. And when someone gets threatened, they usually get a little mean. Do not let these haters stand in your way. Push past them and get the life you want. Saying "no" to your detractors means that you aren't going to let their jealousy make your life miserable. It means that you are going to prevail and you are going to look fabulous while doing it. Hey, you could even take it as a compliment that they're just doing it because they think you're better than them.

Another good point is the point of dealing with other women/hotties. You probably already know that most women are very competitive with other women. I read somewhere once that women don't put on makeup and clothes to really attract males, but they do it to outshine the other women.

Sure, a woman does dress to impress men, too, but that competitive factor is still there, though it may be on a deeply subconscious level. She might not even be aware that she's being competitive either. It's not something she does just to be catty either. It's a biological imperative that has been around since the beginning of time. The more you outshine others, the more potential mates you attract. It's simply about mating and getting her genes into the next generation. In order to do that, she has to look better than her peers. As I've said, it's simply biology.

So, how to deal with other women? Just allow them to do their thing and you do yours. In fact, learn from them. Hotties always have a few tricks up their sleeves that could help a girl.

It's important to always be yourself, just the best version of yourself. Remember, you are confident and secure in yourself and can hang with the best of them.

It's also a good idea to live and let live. And try not to get jealous over other hotties or feel inferior or threatened by them. You are a hottie in your own right and you deserve to attract men like crazy, too.

Who's That Girl?

If you are going to be the best version of yourself you can be, it helps to start channeling that girl of your youth and bringing her to the forefront. Somewhere inside of you the younger, brighter and more joyful version resides and she's dying to get out. So, channel her right now.

What did the younger you really want to do with her life? What did she like to do? Painting? Horseback riding? Trips to the zoo? Traveling the world? Visiting big cities? Bar hopping? Going on cruises to exotic lands? Whatever it is that you once loved, rediscover it and rediscover the joy of being you.

While this may seem silly to some, it is the essence of who we are as women. That younger version of us didn't have the same insecurities or doubts. That young woman knew what she wanted and didn't try to force it. She just took things as they came and was happy being who she was. This is how you can really get the essence of who you really are and all you have to do is tap into what you were once like and bring it forth.

As we grow older, I think we do tend to look back at ourselves and become ashamed of the mistakes we've made. This isn't a good thing to do because it makes us disown a part of ourselves. We think if we "hide" who we are, or who we were, then people will love us more now. Unfortunately, this isn't the case and when you do this you only end up attracting people who expect perfection, some of whom want nothing more than to control you. If you could just take the time now to embrace everything about yourself and start feeling that self-love we all had at one point, you'd find yourself not only happier but more appealing to others, as well. And why is that? How can accepting yourself make you more appealing to a man? Well, it shows that you don't let what's happened in your life drag you down. It shows that you are comfortable with yourself and your past, even the uncomfortable parts. You realize that everything that has happened in your life has contributed to make you into the fabulous person you are now. You adopt a "been there, done that, over it" attitude and you move forward instead of treading water in the past.

Yes, it's true that we've all done things we'd rather have not. We all make mistakes. But that's part of life. You just have to realize that whatever mistake was made was made to bring you to this point. It's there, yes, but it doesn't have to drag you down. Just accept that you are human and humans make mistakes. And move on with it. Moving on will not only help you to become a happier person, it will also help you attract men who are better for you because then you will be attracting men who are like you, who don't hold onto the past and who won't make you pay for mistakes that you may have made before they even knew you. If they get into a relationship with you, it's with you, not your past. These are the men you want to attract, not someone who wants to make you pay for something they had nothing to do with. Once you realize this, you can move on.

But how do you do this? It's easy. Now take the first step and get out your old photo albums or high school annuals and find pictures of yourself. When you look at these younger pictures of yourself, what do you see? Happy? Vibrant? The world on a string? See the light in your eyes and rediscover what you were once looking forward to. And what was it? Going to college? Getting a job and making your own money? Dating lots of interesting guys? What was it that you were after then? Figure it out and see if that's what you want now and if it is, realize that it's more attainable than ever. And, if you've already attained it, congratulate yourself and move on to the next thing with confidence.

Also, look at what you were wearing. I once read that most women are still dressing the way they did in college and, if you think about this, it's probably true. I loved cutoff shorts and t-shirts for sporty weekends and still do. (I gravitate to extremely causal situations.) What did you love? Could you make it work now? Obviously, you're not going to wear short-shorts or bright neon t-shirts, but did you embrace the preppy side of you or the glamorous side or the sporty side? Whatever it was, update it and see if you can make it work now and see if makes you feel more like yourself.

Rediscovering your younger self is a great way to figure out what's really important to you and why it's still important now. You can also discover the happier version of yourself, the one who wanted independence or marriage or to start her own business or whatever. It's vital to tap into this and really work with it. This will give you a sense of excitement as well as a bit of challenge. Remembering what you once held dear and awakening it again means that you still care about yourself and your life and where you're headed.

Always moving forward in life is about rejuvenating yourself, no matter what your age is. It's about finding that inner joy and allowing it to show on your face. When you feel young, you will look younger. It's as simple as that. If you can change your outlook, you can change your life. And this is a good way to start.

The Confident Woman

Confidence matters. A lot. And I mean *a lot*. A woman without confidence is like a hippie without his beads. Or a hamburger without the bun. Or, even, New York without its subways. It just doesn't work. A woman with confidence gets what she wants out of life regardless of whether it's a job or a man. A woman *with* confidence is a woman who has guys literally eating out the palm of her hand. Well, not literally, but you get the point. And that's where you want to be. You want to be that woman that men long for and, oddly enough, it isn't that hard if you get some confidence.

Confidence should be your main goal when you're embarking on self-improvement. I know everyone talks about how important confidence is, almost to the point of becoming redundant, but I want to stress it because without confidence, improving your situation is almost impossible.

So, what is confidence? Confidence is basically having self-assurance. It is about not being insecure. It is having a belief in your ability to succeed at anything you do. And to know that if you don't succeed at something, you will do better next time.

One of the most important aspects about confidence is that it can make you feel secure enough to attempt new things and to try out new ideas. Once you have it, it's like your mind opens up which means your *world* will also begin to open up. You start to see the possibility in everything and limitations don't worry you.

So, how do you get confidence? You start believing in yourself. You stop listening to negative self-talk and by that I mean, whenever you have a self-defeating thought, you push it away and replace it with a more positive thought about yourself. Now, this will take some practice but I think you will find that when you start doing it, you will begin to feel better and better about yourself. And that's the goal.

For example, you might say to yourself, "My skin looks dreadful." Yeah, that's a bummer. You might have a zit or two and, hey, everyone gets them. But instead of making it dismal, replace that thought with, "My skin will look better now that I've started using that new wash." See what I'm getting at? Another example, "My bank account looks like a train wreck." Okay, replace with something like, "Sure, my bank account looks bad right now, but it will look better in the future since I've started to pay off those bills. I might even think about adding more to my savings when I get the funds."

It's that simple and it's that easy. And that little bit of positivity will see you through to your next positive thought and so on and so forth. Soon, if you practice hard enough, you will just automatically start thinking with more positivity. And a positive person is a confident person.

You want to feel empowered, not disempowered. You want to feel strong, not weak. And if it's your thoughts that keep you from feeling these things, then switch them up. It's a tried and true way to gain more self-confidence. From there, just try things that will gain you some confidence. Maybe go to a coffee shop alone if you've never done this. Why not agree to a blind date when someone sets you up? While it may not work out, it means you are taking a bit of a risk and with every risk comes more confidence. And that is what you are after.

If you want more confidence, it's also vital to really start to have fun. Yes, that's right. Having fun isn't just for kids who enjoy going to theme parks; it's for all us grownups, too. Having fun is crucial because it gives you a sense of joy and with joy comes more confidence. And, no, you don't have to visit a theme park in order to have fun. Just have more fun with whatever you're doing.

Some of us don't have much fun because we hate our jobs and our jobs can seem to take up so much of our lives and mental capacity. So, having fun might be hard if you hate your job. If you hate your job, why not try to find a better one? If you can't do that, just let it go and separate yourself from work as much as possible. You can do this by not thinking or talking about it that much when you're away from it. You can shut it out and live a happier life if you make the effort to do so. After you've clocked out, just let it go and move into your day without having it hanging over you. I know a woman who's always obsessing about her job, even when she's at home. It drives her—and me—crazy because that's all she wants to talk about. Well, until she realizes that you have to leave work at work, there's no getting through to her.

Having confidence means you have to believe in yourself. Again: You have to believe in yourself. This means don't let self-doubt ever sabotage any effort you might put forth. This means just doing whatever it is you want to do and hoping for the best results. And, once you get those desired results, you don't have to boast. Showing the world that you're a confident person is bragging enough. If you're hot stuff, everyone will know it. And probably be jealous. So, just smile at your detractors and delight in the fact that they are green with envy at you.

The Not-So-Confident Woman

We talked about confidence in the last chapter, so now I want to focus this chapter on lack of confidence, which can be a big hindrance for a lot of women.

If this applies to you, it's best to ferret out exactly what went wrong and why you now lack confidence. I believe getting to the root of the problem will not only help a girl feel better but will help remedy the problem, as well.

Lack of confidence holds people back in most every aspect of their lives. For women this is a particular hardship because many of us were raised with the belief that we have to have a man to take care of us. Until we can be confident that we can take care of ourselves without a man, we will always have that doubt and that doubt will make us desperate to find a man, any man, to date and eventually marry.

The only way to remedy this lack of confidence, and I've seen it in many women, is to become self-sufficient. This doesn't mean that you become a man-hater or anything like that. It just means that you find a way to make yourself feel more secure. This could be by saving more money, paying debt off or securing a better job. Lack of confidence in women seems to arise from a fear that they won't be able to take care of themselves financially. If you can overcome this, then you will automatically feel more confident.

But without the confidence to actually pursue anything, you might find yourself in a standstill. I've been there and I know many other people who have as well. So, it's essential to find your confidence before you begin whatever it is you're attempting to do. Some people are just lucky and they already have loads of confidence before they do anything.

Most of us aren't like that, though, and we have to try and succeed before we gain confidence. However, if we could just switch it around and find that confidence we need in order to attempt anything, we might find that even if we do fail, we're still okay. So, what keeps us from trying? It's called lack of confidence and it can come in many forms.

One reason for lack of confidence might be that you've been demeaned by others. I know some women who, or whatever reason, just seem to invite people into their lives who want to bring them down. No matter what they do, there always seems to be someone there pointing their finger and telling them that they are failures. Maybe they pick the wrong friends or they're the scapegoat in their family; it doesn't matter. This is not a good situation for anyone to find themselves in. Usually, when this happens, it just means that the other people are somehow threatened by this person and want to level her.

Leveling someone simply means when another person or group of people bring a person down to their level or below so they don't feel so bad about themselves. This is usually accomplished by saying disparaging remarks that undercut a person's self-esteem. Leveling is the one of the worst things a person can do to another human being but it's done all the time, believe me. If this has happened to you and you look back and see a pattern of this, take time to really assess what's going on. Usually, some jealousy is at play and this means that whatever you are doing is somehow threatening to others. No, you're probably not doing anything "wrong," either. What's happening is that many people don't want to put the effort in to succeed at anything and just want to live their lives easily drifting by. When they see someone who steps up to the plate and takes a swing at life, this makes them very uncomfortable. They become threatened and then feel the need to take the person down. Because of that, they want you to step down so that they don't feel inferior. They just want you to give up. The kicker is, they want this without actually having to make an effort to do anything themselves other than putting you down! Ugh! This is enough to drive a person absolutely crazy. But the trick is to beat them at their own game and to cut them off at the pass. The remedy to this is to ignore your detractors. Go on with whatever it is you're doing in order to succeed. *Don't let them stop you.* Successful people are faced with situations like this all the time and have to work hard to overcome them. If you want to be successful and, particularly, if you want to be a hottie, you will have to learn to not let people like this stop you from achieving your goals.

Some say that success is just hard work and not giving up on a goal. I say that is only a part of it. Another part of it that others fail to mention is the part of the detractors. This is where a lot of people get tripped up without even realizing it. Being successful isn't just about working hard and overcoming obstacles. It's about figuring out who is trying to thwart your success and rising above them.

So, it's crucial that you become aware of detractors in your life because they can undermine your confidence like no other. When they do this, you will probably start to feel a lot of self-doubt that you would have otherwise not have felt. If you want to be a hottie or a successful business executive or whatever, then you have to learn to ignore people like this and get on to doing it.

The moral of the story is that there are many things out there that can undermine your confidence. However, they can be overcome if you are just aware of them. Most of it comes from self-doubt that is generated from within due to bad presences and influences in your life. Once you know this, you can more easily make the adjustments you need to your attitude and your confidence can finally begin to grow.

Lack of Self-Esteem

We've established that the biggest factor when it comes to poor self-confidence is a lack of self-esteem. Regardless of the source, it comes from us not liking or loving ourselves. Lack of self-esteem keeps us from trying new things and from being all we can be. It is the root of our dysfunctional relationship with ourselves. We feel as though we aren't worth anything and no one else will find us worthy, either.

What you need to keep in mind is that others do find us worthy, but in order to really get that, we have to first believe in ourselves. This is tricky because without having the approval of others it's hard to find the confidence to believe in ourselves. But that's what we have to do in order to get past the needing approval part because once you stop needing approval from others, you will really start to feel your power. And having confidence is having power and once you've got that, you will be well on your way to succeeding at anything you want.

For some people, their deep-seated lack of self-esteem arises from a childhood of pain. Maybe you were bullied or your parents constantly told you that you were worthless. If this is the case, you might want to get some therapy to help you deal with these issues. If that doesn't sound appealing, why not try to get to it yourself? Why not ask yourself why you lack self-esteem? I'd be willing to bet that you will figure it out in no time and once you do, you will be able to release it. You will be able to let it go. But, most importantly, it will allow you to start loving yourself. You have to realize that, in retrospect, the things that undermined your self-esteem are probably not that big of a deal. They just seemed like it at the time because you were younger and had less experience in the world.

When it comes to low self-esteem, look around at your life and at your relationships. See how they might contribute to it. I once had a friend who always put me down, but did it in a way that was not very obvious to me at the time. It was like she would say things to me but in such a way that it was hard to figure out if it was an insult or not. She took advantage of the fact that I considered her to be a good friend and assumed that she would not treat me like that. She was preying on my good nature but after a while, I was able to figure out what she was doing. She was undermining my self-confidence because the stuff she would say would stick in my head and make me doubt myself. Once I realized what she'd been doing, I had an "a-ha!" moment and was finally able to remove her from my life. Since then, I have been much more confident.

Another thing my "friend" would do whenever I didn't want to do exactly what she wanted was put me down by saying, "You used to be nicer. You used to do anything anyone asked of you." During this time, I was having some health problems and was just so tired I couldn't think straight. Reflecting back, I only wish I'd stood up to her and told her, "Listen, I don't feel good. Just because you want me to do this or that doesn't mean I have to do it. If you were a friend, you wouldn't expect so much and you'd be more understanding."

Now, to any outsider it was fairly obvious what she was doing but my mind was clouded by what I thought was our friendship. But hindsight is twenty-twenty. I don't have much contact with her anymore, mainly because she crossed the line with me one too many times. I didn't expel her from my life or anything but a toxic relationship like the one we had will eventually run its course, and it did.

Let me be clear on this. I am not saying to get rid of everyone in your life. No, no, no. I am simply saying to examine these relationships and if they are too toxic to hold onto, simply start pulling back a little. Obviously, this will be harder with family and you will usually have to make concessions for family that you wouldn't otherwise do for so-called friends. Family is different so if you have problems with them, just reassess and try to really listen to what they are saying and when they say it and try to detach yourself from it. Family can sometimes make you feel bad about yourself, but you don't have to listen! No one has to listen to critics! Do you think Mozart did? No! It's important to realize that a lot of times in families, people put you down without realizing that they are doing it. As you grow up, people fall into roles and sometimes the role is that of the annoying older brother or bitchy younger sister. However, with dysfunctional and undermining people who you aren't necessarily obligated to stay connected to, really pay attention to what they are doing to how you think of yourself. You might realize that putting yourself down stems somewhat from the way others are treating you. Also, look at the lives of these people who put you down. Most likely, you'll find that if you were so inclined, you could find a lot to insult about them as well. So don't listen to or take them very seriously. And give them a smile, too.

Yes, smile at your detractors, at those people who want to make your life a living hell. And you're smiling because you're winning at life and they're losing at trying to make your life hard. Anytime anyone tries to give you a hard time, know that it's usually because they're jealous and don't let it bother you. Just smile and move on from them and become even better.

Once you start finding that you have more confidence, you will become more comfortable in your own skin. This means you will begin to accept everything about yourself. You will learn to love it. And you will learn to really like yourself. And that's the goal, isn't it? The goal is to find your higher self, the one you've squashed in order to appease your detractors, the people who do not have your best interests at heart. The goal is to defeat self-doubt and try your hand at success. It's to overcome any childhood issue that still might be dragging you down. And once you do this, you will find that you are one super confident hottie.

Becoming self-confident means becoming less self-conscious. If you are self-conscious, just stop. Learn how to relax and just go with the flow. So what if you're having a bad hair day? It happens to the best of us. So what if you have a zit on your chin? Who cares? Just smile at the world and you will find that the world will begin to smile back. While you're at it, give it a wink, too.

There's Something About You

While this chapter touches on a subject we discussed earlier, I wanted to go into more detail about it. More specifically, I want to touch on the subject of your one good thing. I also want to emphasize that if you can become really comfortable with yourself, you will inevitably become more comfortable being yourself in public and especially more comfortable around men. And a woman who is comfortable around men is a woman men want to meet and date. She's fun to hang out with, she tells good jokes and she doesn't mind a bit of good-natured teasing. There's just something about her...about you.

Every woman has one good thing that sets her apart from other women. If you think about Hollywood celebrities, each of them has a specific talent or attribute that makes them who they are. Some have the ambition and drive. Some might have a really good butt or pair of legs, or a nice laugh or, even, some talent for acting. The point is, each of these women has something that makes them just a little bit different from everyone else and it rarely has anything to do with looks. The important thing about this is that this principle not only applies to Hollywood celebrities, it applies to you as well.

So, there's something about you that will set you apart from everyone else. What is that something that makes you special? It is a specific trait that only you have. The trick is to find it and exploit it for all its worth. Maybe you're really smart or maybe you have beautiful eyes or maybe you have a talent of some kind—such as playing the accordion or juggling. That may sound silly, but what makes you unique will also make you a hottie that will attract men like crazy.

And once you find that one thing, you just combine it with all your other great attributes and that will make for one cool chick.

One way to get your mind around this to think of the movie *There's Something About Mary*. In this funny film, Mary is a girl that all these guys are absolutely crazy for. What does she have that sets her apart? Well, she's just really cool. Of course, she's pretty and of course she can tell a good joke, but most of all, this girl is confident and is really comfortable around men. She doesn't walk around with a chip on her shoulder or hold grudges about past bad relationships and she doesn't try to hide who she is. She's simply herself and men love her for it.

Obviously, Mary is a fictitious character but she does embody everything guys want in a woman. Of course, it would be ludicrous to suggest for you to take cues from a fictitious character. Or would it? Think about it for a moment. Men really dig women who are cool and who also have something that sets them apart from everyone else. And that's all you have to do in order to attract men. You have to get to a point where you're cool with what's happened in the past, thus letting go of it. This will get you to the point where you believe in and feel good about yourself. And that's pretty much it.

So, find your something special and use it to your advantage. When you do this it will allow you to be yourself. And when you can be yourself, you will be more comfortable around men. It's okay if they like you and it's okay if they don't. You are you and that makes you a genuine hottie. Keep in mind that you don't have to become like Mary. You just have to become yourself. That's all Mary was doing in the movie. She was just being herself and men loved her for it. She wasn't trying too hard. There is a delicate balance and if you can get your head around this, you will be ahead of the game, believe me.

Men love women who are confident and secure in themselves. They love women who aren't like everyone else and that's why you should always aspire to be yourself. Who else would you want to be? If you use your unique talents to your advantage, you will only enhance how great you are.

Even If You Feel Like Being Sloppy, Always Look Your Best

Yes, I understand that sounds like an absolute contradiction in terms, but hear me out. I know that some women like to just throw on any old thing to run to the grocery store or whatever and that's fine. But if you do this, just make sure that your clothes are clean and, even if they look a little sloppy, they should be stylish. You never know who you might run across when you're out and about, so it's necessary to always look like you're pulled together.

You should always look well put together even if you're just going to the gym in sweatpants. If you always take the extra effort to make your outfit into a look, you will attract more attention. However, looking downright sloppy is never an option. So, say for instance, you are going to the gym and just throw on a pair of sweats. Well, the sweats should be clean, free of holes and fit well. Pair this with a cute pair of flip-flops—leave the running shoes in your gym bag—and a pair of stud earrings and a nice, body flattering top. Be sure to pull your hair into a ponytail and, voila! You've got a look.

If you just take that little bit of effort every time you go out, you're probably going to look much better than most. This doesn't mean that you have to dress to the nines if you're just going to get some coffee. But if you do want to wear a pair of sweats, why not throw on a pair that fits well and looks good so that you don't look like you just rolled out of bed? This is an easy fix. Most clothing stores now carry great sweatpants that look cute for running errands or you can wear a pair of leggings with a longer sweatshirt or t-shirt. Throw your hair into a messy ponytail or bun and you will look like a fashionista who can pull any look off, even sweats.

One thing I've noticed lately is that some women are going out in public with their pajamas on. Yes, they might just be going out to breakfast or to the grocery store or whatever, but it always makes me wonder, "Did they just roll out of bed to come here? Did they even brush their teeth?" I just can't get my head around this. Why would someone do something like this? Are they too lazy to put on a pair of pants before they leave the house? And I'm not talking about hopping in the car and going through the drive-thru for coffee. I'm talking about being out in public wearing your beddy-bye clothes. And I know if I'm thinking this, everyone else is too, except the girl wearing them, probably.

Wrong. No. Do not do this. What if you see a really cute guy? You can't go up to him or try to catch his eye. He'll always think of you as the sloppy girl in PJs. So, if you do this, do yourself a favor and stop. While there might be some men who will think this is a cute look because, usually, pajamas are really cute, it's still too sloppy. I'd suggest leaving this look in the hamper.

You should always be ready to attract men, even early in the morning. If you go out looking like hell that will be the one day you see a great guy you can't talk to because, hey, he's going to always remember you were dressed like you came from a slumber party. Get what I'm saying?

So, do yourself a favor and if you want a go-to sloppy look for the weekends or whatever, just buy a cute pair of sweats and flip-flops to pair with a nice t-shirt or whatever. Do a little something to your hair and make sure you've brushed your teeth. Taking just a bit of time to look slightly but coolly sloppy will get your better results than if you just rolled out of bed and went to the store. Trust me on this one. Making an effort always pays off.

Now, some of you might be thinking about the chapter on elegantly disheveled and wondering how I can say this when I said that. Being elegantly disheveled is not about wearing pjs in public. It's not about being sloppy. It's about being casual but stylish and elegant at the same time—like a Birkin bag. So, it's important to realize that whenever you go out, looking your best is a must. You want to project to the world that you're a stylish and fabulous person, not a sloppy one. There is a fine line here, but if you can manage to walk it, you are going to be the envy of women everywhere and the focus of men.

Your Body, Your Self... But Mostly Your Body

The weight issue. That's what we're talking about. I almost hesitate to go into this because so many women have issues with their bodies and I certainly don't want to add to anyone's angst. However, in order to be a hottie, you should try to be in the best shape you can comfortably be.

Let's face facts. Men like women who look good in a short skirt. They also like beer and football. We could take a moment to try and understand this. However, we won't because it's not that important. What's important is that most men are attracted to women who keep themselves in shape. We can all agree on that, right? So, if you're interested in losing weight and getting in shape, read on.

Here's what happened to me. A few years ago, I found myself battling the bulge and could not get the weight to, well, budge. I tried this diet and that diet and almost drove myself insane trying to lose those pounds. Nothing worked, ever. And if it did work, I'd feel pretty terrible in the process. So, I eventually got sick of doing this and got down to the basics. I started cutting back on what I was eating and began to really watch those calories. And it worked. And it still does. But I have to stay vigilant. I still watch what I eat. And I don't eat after dinner. And I also don't snack. And I stay at about the right weight for my height.

If you want to lose weight, it's important to really look at what you're eating. If you are eating a lot of high-calorie junk food, why not try substituting something low-calorie instead like fruit and salads? Also, watch your coffee drinks.

Those things are loaded with calories. Try cutting them out and maybe just drink black coffee instead.

The point is to just look at what you're eating and then try to cut down. If you want to lose weight, this is a fairly fool-proof method. I just wouldn't suggest going on any fad diet. I'd just suggest cutting back on what you're eating now and reducing or eliminating snacks and late-night eating out altogether. That's what really works. That's what's always worked for me, anyway.

If you are really attentive to calories, you can go online and Google "calories needed" and Google will pull up calorie counters. All you have to do is put in your height and how much weight you want to lose and it will tell you about how many calories you need a day in order to lose the amount of weight you wish to lose. This is a fast, easy and effective way to lose weight. And you don't have to give up your favorite foods. All you have to do is cut down on them and count calories, which can be a pain but in the end result is losing weight. No not a bad tradeoff.

What about exercise? Well, I will tell you from my own experience that just exercising won't make you skinny. But it will improve your muscles and make you feel really, really good. So, yeah, it's always a good idea to hit the gym or go for a jog or whatever. The point is to find something you love doing—dancing, running, volleyball—and do that for your exercise. But if you want to lose weight, you will have to adjust your food intake.

The hardest part to losing weight is actually starting. It's hard to take that first step because that means you're committing to it. But if you watch what you eat and exercise some, you can and will lose weight. It's not that hard, either. And the great thing is, once you lose weight, your confidence will soar and you will physically feel so much better.

Keep in mind that I am not an expert and you should consult with a doctor before beginning any new diet/exercise program. Once he/she gives you the go-ahead, go ahead and get that body you've been longing for.

Now, this is what worked for me. However, I am not telling you to lose weight or that you should. I am just telling you what worked for me. If you want to try it, it's up to you but be sure to consult with your doctor before beginning any diet or exercise program.

You've Got Purpose and Goals

You should never sit around and wait for the world to hand you something. More importantly, you should have goals and the confidence to follow through with them. Goals are something every woman should have. Without them, what fun is life? A goal can give your life purpose and direction. It can also give you satisfaction and a tremendous feeling of accomplishment once you've attained it.

A purpose is sort of like a goal but with a broader range. A purpose is a long range goal that is essentially the focus of your life. It is why you do the things you do and how you live your life. Everyone in life has a purpose. The trick is to find yours. And all you have to do is figure out something you really love to do. I am sure you've heard the saying, "Do what you love and the money will follow." While this phrase normally applies to artists and businessmen, you can take it and apply it to anything. Maybe you want to open up your own restaurant. That's a really worthy goal. Maybe you want to be a mom. Good for you! So, take some time and figure out what it is that you love to do. And once you do that, work at trying to attain your goal.

To reiterate: A goal is a singular thing that can be attained and a purpose is more ongoing. So, my advice would be to find a goal you'd really like to achieve and then go for it. Having this goal will give you purpose and having purpose will make for a more satisfying life. Another way to look at purpose is to see it as being sort of like a theme that your life takes. Some people say that their purpose is to be a mother. Others say it's to help others. Usually a goal fits within that purpose and makes life really fulfilling.

Just knowing what you want to do with your life and having a goal will not only boost your confidence, it will give you something to look forward to. And once you achieve it, you will be so satisfied with yourself, your self-esteem will go through the roof.

Of course, achieving your goal might take years, so don't let life hang in the balance while you're working at achieving it. Just work at it and live life while you do so.

Obviously, once you do find your purpose, don't get all single-minded about it and forget about everything else in your life, including being a hottie. It's important to have fun every once in a while and dance the night away. It's important to think about marriage and babies and all that good stuff, as well. But having a goal, a purpose, is the spice of life. This is something just for you. It's all yours, so own it and revel in it. And once you achieve your goal, you will be so proud of yourself. And others will, too.

Along with purpose comes respect. Many people don't respect themselves enough to even admit there's something they'd really love to do. Respect is important. It's important to have and to give. So, learn to respect others but, most importantly, start with yourself. Once you start respecting yourself enough, you will emit an aura that will always allow others to think of you as a person to be highly regarded. By doing this, you are setting yourself up for being someone that deserves not only respect but to achieve their goal. But you have to start with yourself. By doing that, you will find that it will be easier to respect others. This is because you will become more confident and confidence will always radiate from you.

Age Appropriate

If you want to look sexy, it's always a good idea to dress age-appropriately. There is nothing sadder than a woman of "certain" age trying to look like a twenty-year-old except for maybe a twenty-year old dressed like an older woman. (Hey, I've seen it.)

So, it's necessary to dress according to your age. This doesn't mean you can't look stylish or you can't follow trends. It just means you have to adapt what is in fashion to suit your age. If you do this, you don't run the risk of looking a little silly when you're out and about.

If you're not sure what might be age appropriate, just look around at other stylish women your age and see what they're wearing. This doesn't mean if you're a little older that you have to dress in a skirt suit and pearls, either. You can still look hip as long as you forgo the belly-baring t-shirts and the super-short minis. Of course, this is just common sense. Most people know when something is too young for them or too old, unless they are completely oblivious, that is.

A good rule of thumb for any age group is this: If you sit down and your skirt shows the world the color of your underwear, it's too short. It's about looking classy, not trashy. So find things that accentuate the positive aspects of your figure and leave the others for someone else. Hopefully, they will bypass them as well.

Dressing age appropriately will have benefits other than making you look good. It will also make you more confident and enable you to attract a better quality of men. This is because you will be attracting men who are attracted to you not because you're trying to be something you're not, but because you're being you. And that's the best thing you can be.

Say What You Mean and Know What You're Saying

One thing that can make a girl seem not so smart is the mispronunciation or misuse of words, especially fifty-cent words, as they say. I speak of this from experience. And, yes, it's very embarrassing. If you don't know how to pronounce something, just don't use it in conversation until you learn how to say and use it correctly. If you do this, you will look like a true bona fide smarty pants. Hey, it's better than looking like the alternative.

I mention this because I've seen women slip up and almost die of embarrassment when they're called out on this issue. And, yes, it's happened to me. So, if you want to use big words, do so, but just make sure you're using them correctly as well as pronouncing them correctly. And while this may seem embarrassing, wouldn't it be better to hear it here rather than from some guy you're trying to impress? I think so.

Another note on the topic: It's never a good idea to use words that aren't real or are nonstandard. And we all know what this means. For some reason the nonstandard word "irregardless" is used like it is, in fact, a real word. (The word everyone is actually looking for here is "regardless.") It's not. Look it up if you don't believe me. If you're not sure if a word you're using is nonstandard, always look it up. And as far as slang goes? It's cool and hip to use it, but never to overuse it.

Knowing your stuff when it comes to vocabulary will not only impress any man you run across, but it can come in really handy during a job interview. So, jump to the front of the class and don't be afraid to look smart. Just don't look dumb but using or pronouncing words incorrectly.

Remember, you want to look cool and collected, not dumb. If you don't have to risk it, then why risk it? Yes, some people in this world might equate being cute as being dumb, but let that be their folly. If you keep yourself in check on this matter, you will not only look smarter in the end, but you will appear to be a fun, hot chick. And when you can slip in a fifty-cent word correctly, then do so. That will only add to your aura of confidence and competence.

Choose for Yourself

One thing that women who are successful and confident in dating do is that they choose the men they date and eventually marry. They don't leave it to chance. They don't get desperate and go out with just any dude that asks them to dinner. If they don't like a certain man "in that way" they don't waste their time. *See ya, buddy!*

If you find that you're dating men that don't really do it for you, it might be because you feel anxious about finding a man and getting into a committed relationship. In other words, you might be doing this because you're desperate. We've already discussed this, but let's touch on it for a moment here, too.

Some women think if they wait too long then they'll end up alone. Hey, it's a legitimate fear. But it's just a fear. You can get over this if you just realize that you're not waiting for Mr. Perfect; you're waiting for Mr. Perfect *for you.* I know that doesn't take away the sting of having to actually wait, but it's better to wait than to marry just anybody because he's the one that asked first. But that was your old attitude. Becoming a hottie entails getting a new attitude and part of that attitude is knowing that you can and will find the right man for you.

Keep in mind that the right man will not be perfect, as none of us mere mortals are. What you want is someone you can relate to that can relate to you. You want to be attracted to him yet you still want him to be down to earth enough so you can have a rapport. Also, you're looking for a guy that has the same goals as you, whether it's to be independently wealthy, having a family or to travel the world. Whatever your goals are, they should somewhat match the goals of your paramour.

Yes, that might seem like a tall order, and you can adjust it accordingly, but the point is, that you don't have to settle. Sure, not all men are perfect, as I said, but settling for someone just because he's a man and he's breathing is selling yourself short. It's also being desperate. And that's no way for a hottie to be.

If you wish to not sell yourself short, one of the main ways to do this is to distinguish yourself from others. This will put yourself in the position of choosing your date. That's right. You have to put yourself in the position of the chooser. That means, you choose who you go out with. Just because some guy who's "pretty good" asks you out and you don't have a date for Saturday night, you don't accept unless you really like the guy and could see yourself spending some quality time with him. If you're unsure? It wouldn't hurt to go out with him and see if you click. If not, there's no need for a second date. Having this attitude puts you in charge.

By allowing yourself to be in charge of your own life, instead of at the mercy of men, you will be in a better position for possible love connections. Seriously, you will. If you date some guy just to be dating him, you're not being a hottie, but a girl who thinks she's not good enough to get the guy of her dreams.

If you know that it's okay to wait for the right guy and that you will find him eventually, you're not off-setting any chance you might have with this or that guy, but increasing your odds. If you waste your time dating men you don't much like, you are blocking potential love connections from happening. And why is this, you ask? It's because most men will not infringe on what they think is an existing relationship. If you're wasting your time on a man who isn't doing it for you, other men will think you're in a serious relationship. It's too much trouble to get involved. What if your boyfriend is a psycho? It happens, believe me. Most men do not want that hassle.

This is why you have to put yourself into the position of being the chooser. This doesn't mean walling yourself off from all men. This doesn't mean never going on a date while you're waiting for Mr. Perfect. What it means is being available when the right guy comes along and if you're involved with Joe Schmo who's not really someone you even like, then you're not going to be available. And he's going to walk right past you.

But it's important to allow it to happen and to not force it. And you don't have to wait for those attractive men to come to you, either. You can always go after them. No, you're not going to chase him down but rather you go after him more subtly; you're simply going to let him know you're interested. And how do you do that? You can say hello or smile at him. You can even ask him out yourself, though I only suggest doing this in cases of extreme shyness or stubbornness on the part of the man. (Asking a man out is a tricky situation. We'll discuss this more in-depth later.)

A note: believe it or not, some really hot guys are so unaware of their hotness that they will not make a move until a woman does it first. This could be you. Just do it in a subtle way and score yourself a hottie!

Initial attraction is almost instantaneous. It's not something you really have to think about. Either you have it or you don't. Sometimes it can grow but usually not if you're not attracted from the get-go. If this is the case, you'll know it. And so will he. So, if you are attracted to a guy, then allow that attraction to happen. Once you feel it, if he's attracted to you, he will feel it too. And then you two can come together. It's important at this stage to not over-think it, either, but to allow nature to take its course. And by relaxing into the process, you will find that you attract all kinds of men, even a few with whom you might want to settle down with.

Once you learn to wait for that initial attraction, you will automatically set yourself up for better dating, and then better relationships. It's just being willing to give yourself over to the process and learning how to navigate the world of dating. It's about allowing yourself the freedom of choosing whatever man it is that you want to be with, not allowing the choice to be made for you. It's about not settling, but about getting what you want—within reason—and living the life as only a hottie can.

Getting Your Man

When a confident woman and sexy wants a man, she's going to get him. This isn't to say that she's going to break up any existing relationships, either. But she's not going to hesitate to go for what she wants and if it's a man, she's going to get her man.

And how does she do it? Well, she knows her worth and has the confidence to go for what she wants, that's how. She knows that she deserves what she wants and knows that she's capable of getting it.

And this is how you have to be. You have to feel that you are quite capable of landing the man of your dreams. You have to feel that no matter what, if there is a man you'd like to have as your own and that you have the power to go out and get him. You have to feel the empowerment we talked about earlier that all women possess. You have to embrace your hotness. And, lastly, you have to be yourself.

So, how do you get this confidence you need in order to go after what you want? Well, first, you should make yourself available. You should never hide yourself or your power. You aren't waiting for some man to "discover" you or, for that matter, for a man to ride up on a white horse. You should not be in fantasy land. You should be in reality. And being in reality means that you are available to the available men in your area and being available means you're going to be wanted.

Of course, being available means that *you* know you're available. That you know what you're looking for and are open for people who are looking for someone like you. However, it doesn't mean to broadcast your availability. If you do that, you might look a little *too* available and that's not what you want. You're wanted and that means you're in demand. So, while you know that you are open to new suitors, you don't tell the world this. When you see an attractive man you'd like to get to know better, then you send out a vibe inviting him into your world. You do this with a smile or a hello.

If you're not sure about how to send out a vibe, or it makes you slightly incomfortble, just know that it's easy. All you're doing is establishing contact with him, just like you would with any other human being. If you're attracted, there will probably be a connection. You're a woman. He's a man. This is how it works. You just have to be confident.

Basically, all you're doing is locking eyes briefly with this guy and giving him a slightly interested smile. If he feels like you're someone he'd like to get to know better, he will approach you. If not, he might be confused and look away. (Or he could be shy, busy, have something on his mind, etc.) If this happens, just test the water. Get up and go near him, then find a reason to speak to him, like asking him what time it is because your watch isn't working. (Of course, it probably is working; this is just your excuse to talk to him.) And then you wait on him to start talking. If you feel the interest, engage in conversation and then proceed. He will either ask you for your number or not. And if he does, he's in your world. He's joining you, not the other way around. This means you are in control and are calling the shots.

Remember, if he's available, i.e. not in a relationship, he will want to get to know you better. (Of course, if he is in a relationship, he might be interested, too. I'd just watch this, if I were you, as you don't want jealous ex-girlfriends to become the bane of your existence.) But you might have to nudge him a little in some cases. And you may have to do this because there are men who are basically clueless and have to be nudged in order for them to understand that there's someone interested in them. This means all you have to do is let him know that it's okay for him to ask you out. If he still doesn't, then ask him out—for coffee or a drink. Never for a date. And when you go for coffee or a drink, the ball is in his court. If he doesn't pick it up, then he's going to be benched. It's that simple. You can take a man to water, but you can't make him drink. If he's so daft that he doesn't get what you're doing—trying to start a relationship or just getting to know him better—he needs to not just be benched, he needs to be retired. If this happens, it's time to move onto a man who actually has a clue.

You should never waste time. In certain cases, if a man isn't responding the way you would like, just give up on him and move on. It shouldn't be too much like work. If it becomes work and not fun, take a breather and regroup. If it gets too hard, then learn to back off and let go until you can go back in with a clear head. There is a knack to this and the more you do it, the more success you will experience. You can't lament "the one that got away," either. That's just wasting time. Being a hottie is about being empowered and taking matters into your own hands. It's not about sitting around waiting for some bozo to call. That would kind of defeat the purpose of being a hottie, wouldn't it?

Getting a man is simple. So, don't overcomplicate it. Just get out there and go with the flow. If you see a man you'd like to get to know better, send out that vibe. If he doesn't bite, check his vitals to make sure he's alive, and then proceed. If he turns out to be an idiot—and a lot of them are—just move on and go to the next one until you find the one that's right.

It's that simple. By doing this, you are showing men that you're in control and if they want to join your party, then they're going to have to be up to snuff. Never take on losers and if you find yourself doing just that, you're fighting a losing battle. A loser will always drag you down with him. This is why having absolute confidence in yourself is so vital. It's important because if you can inspire it in yourself, then you can inspire it in others. And if you can inspire it in a man, you are on your way. This means you can make him a better man without even doing anything. That's because you're so hot and attractive and cool, being with you will make him want to be hot and attractive and cool. He thinks some of what you've got will rub off on him.

Finding Fulfillment on Your Own

One thing that a lot of women do is sit around and wait for the perfect man to come into their lives to take care of them. While we discussed this earlier, I wanted to touch on another aspect of this and that is finding fulfillment on your own. I think it's important to learn how not only to stand on your own two feet but to also take care of your own problems. If you don't do this, it's like you're expecting someone else to come in and take care of everything for you. Not a situation any smart woman would want to find herelf in. If you learn to take care of your problmes, you might find that you attract men with little to no problems of their own. This means, the both of you will automatically have more fun together. And a good way to start this process is to look for and find self-fulfillment on your own. Not only will this make you an even more interesting person, it will also make your life that much sweeter. Finding fulfillment means finding things that inspire you or that you simply love to do because you just love to do them. It might be volunteering at an animal shelter or riding a horse or learning to paint. Anything that you can think of that brings you a personal sense of satisfaction means you are on the right track to self-fulfillment. And that's a great place to find yourself.

On the other hand, waiting for someone to come in and take care of your problems or to fulfill you is not a good way to be. I mean, what if your knight in shining armor never shows up? Where would you be then? This is not a predicament any smart woman would want to find herself in, to say the least. Learning how to do things for yourself also means learning how to stand on your own two feet. Doing this gives you a greater sense of self and a terrific feeling of independence. So, it's advisable to take care of your own business before inviting a man, or anyone else for that matter, into your life. Doing these things on your own broadens your sphere of consciousness and really gives your life zest.

So, learn how to take care of business by yourself and when you find someone to share your life with, you're already set in that department.

Also, keep in mind that no one in this world can make you happy, nor is it their responsibility to. That is up to you. While men can and do add to our lives, finding fulfillment on our own only make what they contribute that much sweeter.

Don't Be a Doormat

Granted, women who are considered to be hotties usually have high expectations and they typically don't take any crap. This is good. I don't think any woman should ever take any crap from any man, but that's beside the point. What women should do, though, is expect to be treated well and fairly. That means never become any man's doormat.

Being a doormat for a man, or for anyone else, even family members, is like saying to the world: "It's okay. Go ahead and step on me. I don't mind." Now, you may feel differently about this subject but in my opinion, that's just the way it is. Be that as it may, the kicker is, you don't *have* to be anyone's doormat. Learn how to stand up for yourself and stop being a doormat. If someone is giving you a hard time, call them on the carpet for it. Or, if they're not worth your time, let it go and ignore them. That is, if it isn't bothering you. If it is, talk to them and try to get it ironed out. If nothing else, at least they know you've got their number.

When it comes to men, let them know from the get-go that you are not ever going to let them walk all over you. If you start seeing a guy who doesn't call when he's supposed to or blows you off for whatever reason, call him out or dump him. Do not waste time trying to figure this dude out. Just call him up, ask him what's going on and when he uses some lame excuse tell him, "Well, see ya!" And hang up. That's the only way to deal with men like this. If they want to be jerks, fine, they can go jerk someone else around. Don't wait on some guy to call and don't let him lie about when he's going to call, either. So, if this happens to you, call him out. What do you have to lose? A loser that will do nothing but give you a hard time and some pain to go along with it? No thanks. Bye-bye, chump!

What's most important is that when you start dating someone, don't make him the focus of your life. Let him wonder what's going on with you. You don't have to treat him like dirt, but don't treat him like he's your master, either. I figure, until he's given you a ring, all bets are off. Seriously, until he's ready to really commit, then why be at his beck and call? What good will it do you? The answer is not much.

And the great thing about this is that once you show him you don't need him, he will usually come running because he's afraid you're going to find someone else. Pretty funny how that works, huh? But that's just the way it is.

When you're looking for a man, look for someone who wants the same things as you and won't play games. You don't have to waste your time with jerks that are only out for a good time or whatever. And a new guy doesn't have to come with all the bells and whistles but he can't come in thinking he's your everything. No self-respecting hottie would put up with this.

Stand Up For Yourself

Men like strong women. Well, let me rephrase that—some men like strong women. This doesn't mean you have to berate a man or make fun of him behind his back or whatever. But it does mean to not be afraid to stand up to him. Men like spunk. And what's not to like? If you come across as a church mouse, then how will he ever notice you? But a woman who's not afraid to call bullshit or tell it like it is, is a woman many, many men love to be around.

However, this should always come from a place of confidence. If you're doing it because of some sort of insecurity, then it will show. If a man senses this, he will be put off. When I say to show some spunk, I don't mean to be a bitch. Being a bitch in a relationship comes from a place of desperation and that's never a good place to come from. It's all about having the confidence to show you won't let anyone walk all over you and that you respect yourself enough to stand up for yourself. That's all it is. You just have to be cool, calm and collected and tell him that you're not happy with what he did. That's pretty much it.

Of course, a delicate balance must be maintained. When you stand up for yourself, it doesn't give you a free pass to act like a raving bitch. No, no and no. This means when your guy—or any guy—gives you a little crap, you just don't take it. He should be called out for trying to make you feel bad or embarrassing you or whatever. Just don't let him put you down. You have to know when to hold back and when to let him have it. Don't ever just out and out accuse him of anything or freak out on him. That's not being a strong woman. That's being kinda crazy. But there will be times when he steps out of line, sometimes when he steps *way* out of line, that you need to call him on it, lest you become the aforementioned doormat. Just make sure you do it in a measured and cool way.

Remember, it's all about confidence. Men love women who are confident. Make a bitchy remark but don't go overboard. Men like women who aren't afraid to stick up for themselves.

The point is to speak your mind but don't necessarily go off on him like a crazy person. Allowing yourself to vent on him isn't the idea. But allowing yourself to talk about how you feel—without having an emotional breakdown—is the surefire way to a man's heart. He will know that not only are you a major hottie, but you're a pretty cool girl, too.

A Great Sense of Humor

It's good to have a great sense of humor and if you can make a man laugh, you will have him eating out of the palm of your hand.

One thing that sets many women apart is their great sense of humor. Learning to develop a great sense of humor is one of the best things you can do to move forward and attract men like crazy. When you do this, you are showing the guy you're with that not only can you take it, you can dish it out too. And being a little sassy is something that makes men weak in the knees.

And all it takes is not taking yourself too seriously. It's about realizing and enjoying the moment. It's about getting the joke even if it might be on you. Learning to let loose and learning to laugh at yourself and at life can be a sure-fire way into a man's heart.

Again, as with being a strong woman who doesn't take anything off anybody, a delicate balance must be maintained. While you may learn to poke fun or and tease men at whim, it's never a good idea to go for the jugular and actually make fun of him. Even if you want to. Teasing is also good but you have to stay from hurting his feelings. Tease about things like the lipstick on his cheek after you've kissed him hello, or the way he has to call his mother every Sunday. Tease him about that lock of hair that always falls into his eyes, but not about his bald-spot. It's never a good idea to tease anyone about something they really have no control over. Again, a balance must be maintained. The key is to never tease about anything too serious or that is probably a source of low self-esteem for him. Tease about cute things like dimples or his sheepish smile, and do it in a friendly, sexy way.

One thing, though. It's never a good idea to tease sexually. Yes, you can use innuendo if you really want to get him pumped up but, unless you plan on taking it home, don't go overboard. Men take things literally and if you tease about sexual things, they will think you want to jump in bed. So, if you don't, it's best to leave this until you are ready to take that leap of faith.

But getting back to humor. Like I said, having a great sense of humor is one of the best traits you can develop. A wry, even dry, sense of humor is what you're after. It will enable you to really move forward not only with men but in life. Everyone wants to be around someone who can make them laugh. Learn to develop your sense of humor and see how easily you can win someone over. The key is to loosen up and develop your sense of humor, which may be more dry or low-key. Even if you have a hard time with humor, as long as you go with the flow and smile, you will be likable. Not everyone has to be funny, but it is important to have a sense of humor about life and not take things or yourself too seriously. Otherwise, it might just drive you crazy.

So, practice it, learn to do it and have men falling at your feet. Everyone likes the girl who isn't afraid to make someone laugh and men especially like the hottie who can bring a blush to their cheeks. But use it with caution and with diligence. You don't want to embarrass him or tease mercilessly. That's not funny to anyone.

Treat Him Like a Man

As Coco Chanel once said, "As long as you know men are like children, you know everything." I think she had an excellent point.

Seriously. While, on the surface, men are men and they want to be treated as such—they're big, strong and really charming—below the surface is that little boy waiting for a pat on the head from his mother. I know that sounds strange, but it's true. Men, on the whole, want a woman who can cook them dinner, rock their world in the bedroom and make them feel important. A tall order, I'm sure, but if you can find a way to manage this, you will have the keys to the kingdom and any man you desire.

So, if you want to get to know how men operate, the best thing you can do is try to figure them out. How do they think? (Like a man.) What makes them tick? (Money, sex and usually sports. Oh, and let's not forget beer and porn.) Why don't they understand women? (Because they're men.)

In other words, men aren't really that hard to figure out. They have basic needs and they want those needs met. I say this as a generalization because obviously we all know a few high-maintenance men. But let's just assume, for argument's sake, that the men you will be interested in are just normal guys with normal wants and needs.

One mistake that many women make is that they don't realize is that men don't want anything to be too easy. That's why they refuse to stop and ask for directions. They'd be admitting they don't know something and men hate to do that. They would rather challenge themselves and figure it out on their own. That's just the way they are. If men weren't like this, we'd probably never landed one on the moon or have invented light beer. So, while it's an annoying trait, it's one that helps us to keep going. Women know when it's time to stop and ask for directions. Men don't. They like figuring stuff out on their own. This fits into their biological makeup as the natural aggressors and explorers they are.

We can ascertain that men love a challenge. That's easy enough to understand. Therefore, if you don't pose somewhat of a challenge for him, then he's probably not going to be that interested in you. It's almost necessary that you play hard to get; just don't play impossible to get. Give him a little insight about you at first, but don't open the door all the way. When he calls for a date, don't be too eager. Tell him you'll have to check your schedule and then get back to him. Or you can wait a few hours to call him back. Yes, you do run the risk of him not calling back, but guess what? You can call him back. And if he gets away? He must have been pretty darn skittish, don't you think? And any guy who's that skittish isn't a guy you'd want to keep company with, believe me. If you can hold back and let him do his own thing, this will keep him guessing about you, trying to figure you out. And you will become a mystery to him and men love mystery.

This is a hard call, I know. So, how do you let him know you're still interested while retaining an air of mystery that will ensure your place in his heart? Easy. Just give him enough to stay interested in you. Let him know you like him—without actually coming out and telling him—without letting him know you like him too much. If you're all over him at first, he's going to flee as it's in his nature to reject anything that's too easy. Smile at him, let him ask you out and be nice. But don't overcompensate for anything. Don't gush over him and don't tell him how wonderful it is to finally date someone like him. Just sit back, relax and let him romance you. It's his part to play, after all. He is the chaser and you are the chase.

Before we move on, let me clarify something. There is a distinct difference between mystery and secrecy. If a woman actually lies to a man about things, it will not go well once the truth comes out. Mystery is withholding and gradually revealing. Secrecy is lying and sneaking. Of course, this doesn't mean you have to make a list of all the things you've done in your past and present them to him. It just means never out and out lie about something. Relationships are built on trust, and if you trust your guy enough, he'll be able to handle anything you throw at him. Just pick and choose your battles carefully.

Another important rule is to never make excuses for yourself around a guy you really like. Don't apologize for your job or your weight or the fact that you haven't had a "real" date in a while. You want him to think that you're just going out with him to pass the time, to see what he's like. He can't ever think he's your last resort—ever! If you do this, he won't be anything to you but out the door. Remember, you are a hottie and hotties don't fall all over themselves for any man. Let him do the falling. Remember, all you need is confidence in yourself in order to do this.

In the end, it's easy to understand men. Yes, they are like little boys who want that approval from mom, but they are also big, strong men. Let him know you think he's strong—men love this! And keep in mind that no matter what you do, he's probably going to be perplexed by you and the rest of the women in the world, as well. Men do try to figure us out, but it's a good thing to never allow them to be too successful. Therefore, it might be a good idea to realize that even though they say they do, men don't really want to figure women out. They want mystery, an allure and if they know every single detail about our lives, we'd get pretty boring pretty quickly. That's why it's important to hold back from telling a guy—or anyone for that matter—all the little details of your life. Too much information is just that—too much.

Overall, men are fairly simple and straightforward unless, of course, they're sociopaths but that's another story entirely. Once their needs are met, they are usually pretty happy. You just have to take it on a case by case basis and figure out what needs he has and if you'd be willing to meet them.

Past Lovers

I know some people think that retaining an air of mystery went out with petticoats and ice cream socials, but I think this is the best device you can use to get and keep men. I briefly spoke of this in the last chapter, but I want to reiterate it here because I do believe it is an important point to make: Retain an air of mystery.

When you first go out with a guy, he will most likely want to know every single thing about you all at once. Don't give in to ego and tell him everything. Like I said, it's best to keep a lid on the small details of your life.

And what if he wants to know about your past lovers? Oh, yes, this will eventually come up. He will want to know how many people you've slept with. To me this is a very personal question and it's really no one's business. If he brings it up, why not tell him this isn't the time to discuss your previous love life?

A lot of women have a few—or even more than a few—"mistakes" in their lives they'd rather forget. So, I say, forget about it and don't bring them up to any new man who you might want to date seriously. If you've had more than your fair share—and some of the rest of the worlds too—that's your business. Men will always get pissed off at whatever number you give them. But of course, you can't get away with telling them you're a virgin, can you? No, you cannot.

What to do? What to do? Really, it's just none of his business. To me, it's almost a red flag if he continues to bring it up, especially in the early stages of a relationship. Perhaps discuss his reasons for wanting to know so badly. Obviously, he's the one with the problem.

But the call is yours. Just keep in mind that full disclosure on certain subjects might not be the best call. Just know that this subject will eventually come up and when the time is right, tell it like it is, with one caveat—if you are comfortable telling, that is. If you are not comfortable, just don't get too specific. What he doesn't know won't hurt him. However, if you take this route, just don't demand full disclosure from him either.

Anti-Feminist?

And this brings me to my next point. Is being a hottie anti-feminist? No! Absolutely not. I think hotties are actually more feminist than a lot of women in their thinking because they are using their God-given female attributes to better their lives. We never think to judge someone who's using their intelligence to get a better job or whatever, do we? No, and I don't think we should judge women who get ahead by using their feminine wiles, either.

I believe that some women don't use their femininity because they believe it goes against their feminist beliefs. I don't agree with this. I don't think that we have to look or act like men in order to get ahead. We can be ourselves and part of being ourselves is acknowledging that we are, in fact, women.

Women are not the same as men and we shouldn't try to act like we are. We have different needs, different views and certainly different hormones. We should be proud of everything that makes us women. We should celebrate the fact that we were born female. In my opinion, this does not contradict anyone's feminist beliefs.

Cultivate Yourself

In my opinion, you should always be curious to learn about new, exciting things. Pushing yourself to know more about the world not only awakens a great sense of wonder, it gives you much knowledge and power. You can do this by cultivating yourself. Or educating yourself, if you prefer.

So, how do you cultivate yourself? Basically, you go back to school without actually going back to school and you learn all the things they never bothered to teach you. All you have to do is pick your favorite subjects. It's about opening yourself up to the finer things in life. It's about experiencing new ideas and cultures. It's about broadening your horizons and making yourself a more knowledgeable person.

Say, for instance you always wanted to learn how to play guitar—or piano or the cello or whatever. If you wish to cultivate yourself, this is a great place to start by learning an instrument. Perhaps you veer more towards the finer art of painting and sculpture. Or you want to learn to work with clay or in the garden. Whatever it is, figure out the subject in which you're most interested and then all you have to do is cultivate it. And this is easy to do. All you have to do is read up on the subject or take a class and learn to actually garden or play the guitar or whatever.

From there, it's a good idea to visit places like museums or vineyards, things that are a little off your grid right now that appeals to you. Whenever you think of going on vacation, why not think in more grandiose terms? There are all kinds of good deals on traveling to Europe available. Even if that's not something that you can afford right now, go online and look at these sites and see what it would be like to visit Paris or Barcelona or London. And if you're in Europe? See what it would feel like to visit America, Australia or China or whatever region of the world that really intrigues you.

Also, learn to sample finer foods. Try a French restaurant and sample the menu. Read foodie magazines and go to wine tastings. In addition to these things being loads of fun and very good for your cultivation purposes, you might meet a new man or two. And the great thing about meeting men at places like this is that they probably already have some sophistication themselves and will automatically be interested in the newbie—you—who's learning new things.

Another good way to increase your knowledge is the most obvious—read books. And not only the type of books you've always read, but books on art and architecture and biographies of people who fascinate you. Read books written by humorists and read books with different world views. Reading books opens your mind up to new worlds and it can really help your brain get buzzing with new possibilities. And, additionally, reading books is fun.

I guess the point is to really and truly open your mind to all the possibilities that life has to offer. Being a hottie doesn't mean playing dumb. It means using the world to your advantage to have a great life and find a great man. And, while you're doing it, it means having lots of fun.

Being the hottie that you already are means becoming a well-rounded person who is always eager to keep learning new things. This keeps you active and helps you to avoid becoming stale. And stale is never on the menu.

Take Heartbreak in Stride

We've all had a few failed love relations that, if we're honest with ourselves, were probably doomed from the start. Perhaps they were long distance relationships or based entirely on sexual attraction or we were just in it because the guy was so darn cute. I personally know many women who are still pining for the one that got away. They never move on and keep themselves from enjoying life. This is a very unfortunate way to spend your time. There are plenty of other fish in the sea, after all.

If you are feeling heartbreak from a previous love, why not do yourself a favor and move forward? I know heartbreak sucks. Having a relationship fail makes a girl feel, well, like a failure. But you can overcome that and you do this by starting to feel better right now.

And how do you start to feel better? You can do many things like throwing yourself into your work. Or you can start cleaning out the clutter in your home and getting it neat and tidy. I know that sounds strange to do work to make yourself feel better, but have you never heard the old adage, "Hard work dispels worry?" It's true. Hard work does dispel worry and when you get your mind off your woes, even if for a few hours at a time, it gives you distance from that depressing feeling of heartache. It also gives you a sense of purpose and when you finish, you have tangible evidence of all the hard work you have completed. This is very important on a psychological level.

Sure, sure, you are probably lamenting what you did wrong in the relationship. Did you suffocate him by loving him too much? Make too many demands? Was there someone else? Could you have been around more? Could you have been more available to him and his needs? Could you have been better in bed? Yes, these are all relevant questions but they have absolutely nothing to do with where you are now in life. That time is over and while it is unfortunate, take a stand today to not waste one more minute thinking about some guy with whom you're no longer in a relationship.

He wasn't worth your time. He's gone now. Sucks to be you, I know, but that's how it is. If you want to be happy, you have to learn to take heartbreak in stride and if you can do that, you can get past heartache to get to some good love. And that's the point of overcoming hurdles to live a great life that includes good men who will end up being better for you in the long run.

Heartbreak is a true bitch but you know what else it is? It's a real time waster. We waste so many hours and days and months of our lives agonizing over what could have been. If only we could open our eyes to the possibilities of what could be, we could turn it around. And that's what you have to do—just open your eyes and let the sun shine in. Yeah, you know that old song, right? "Let the sun shine in; face it with a grin…" And that's what you have to do. Let go of that dude who broke your heart and face the day with a smile. And when you start smiling at the world, you might just find that it returns the favor.

Override Everything With Gratitude

This may or may not be how all hotties think, but I think they should. Now I know you probably don't like being told what to do but just listen. Whatever you are feeling right now, take a moment and override it with gratitude. Any time you feel something negative, think of something positive and say thanks. Quietly, in your mind, push that negative thought out and literally say thank you for something in your life that you appreciate. And it could be anything—your verve, your intelligence, your family, perhaps the amount of money you've been able to save. Maybe you really dig your TV or car. Whatever it is, say thank you.

Gratitude will not only make you feel like a better person, but it allows better things and more abundance into your life. It also helps get you out of a negative state of mind and helps you to see that while there are bad things about your life that you don't like, there are also good things that you do appreciate. Obviously, this goes along with the Law of Attraction and that's okay. I think it's a very good mindset to develop.

You Were Always a Hottie

Truly becoming the hottie you already are isn't that difficult. But it might entail stepping out of your comfort zone. But, hey, that's life and hotties know how to live life. In fact, they just don't live it, they devour it. So, starting today, devour something. Enjoy it. Bask in the glow of feeling satisfied. Find not only your inner peace, but your inner hottie. And she's in there, just waiting for you awaken her.

The main point of this book is to not turn you into a hottie, as I believe most women are already hotties, if they would only allow themselves to be. The main initiative of this book is motivation. If you can just take something from this and get motivated, you will be on your way. What I want to stress, in the end, is that if you lack that initial motivation, nothing will come of this. So, I hope this book has sparked that in you. Getting motivated to be the hottie you are will make you feel good. And it will bring many new possibilities into your life.

All women are hotties, if only we would begin to believe it. We have the innate ability to attract any man we want. We have the strength and power of our feminine wiles to see us over any heartbreak, any disappointment in life. We have the ability to get anything we want out of life. And the first step in doing this is beginning to believe in yourself. With belief in yourself, you can gain the confidence to overcome any obstacle to get the life you so desire. But it does entail taking that first step. So, step up and take a swing at life. It's waiting for you.

Be the hottie you already are but haven't allowed yourself to be. And be willing to let life be what you want. All it takes is letting go of resistance and overcoming futility. All it takes is a desire to get what you want. And, as we've learned, hotties always get what they want.

So, go get it.